The Three Seas
Roland W. Abbott

© 1987, Roland W. Abbott

All rights reserved. No part of this work covered by the copyrights hereon may be reproduced or used in any form or by any means—graphic, electronic or mechanical—without the prior written permission of the publisher. Any requests for photocopying, recording, taping or information storage and retrieval systems of any part of this book shall be directed in writing to the Canadian Reprography Collective, 214 King Street West, Suite 312, Toronto, Ontario M5H 2S6.

Cover photo: The schooner *Mollie*

∝ Printed on acid-free paper

Published by
RJ BOOKS
P.O. Box 8660, St. John's, Newfoundland A1B 3T7

Printed in Canada by:
ROBINSON-BLACKMORE PRINTING & PUBLISHING

1st printing March, 1987

2nd printing March, 1995

ISBN 0-920884-16-4

The Three Seas

Roland W. Abbott

RB Books
St. John's, Newfoundland

THE THREE SEAS

I called this book **THE THREE SEAS** because the schooners in the three short stories were destroyed by heavy seas.

Now, no doubt it took more than three seas to completely wreck the vessels, but there's something notable about three seas.

When I was a boy fishing with my father and brothers on the Offer Wadhams Island, there was a rock off the Tickle (harbour), just under the water surface which would break in heavy sea. That is, the sea would cover the rock with turbulent waters. No boat would venture in or out while that prevailed.

However, after the sea broke over the rock three times in succession it became calm or much smoother. Then the boats would be able to go in or out as desired, until the next three seas.

Old fishermen and sailors experienced the same at sea. Three big waves, then a smoother ocean surface. That's the tides in sequent motion. They advised one to "wait for three seas". Like the maxim: "After the storm comes the calm".

Truly, it is the same that took its toll of all three vessels, and the crews of two, the "Rudolph" and "Mollie". Thus, as I wrote of them a thought came to me like this:

Once Seas: At Northern Head, nineteen hundred twenty-six,
                The "Ella M. Rudolph" now we see;
            Lost eight of her crew
                In a mighty great sea.

Seas Again: When nature and elements were not too kind,
                Destroyed the "Erema H."
            With seas in nineteen hundred, twenty-nine.

Three seas: On a dark stormy night,
                When that angry sea;
            Smashed to matchwood
                The schooner, "Mollie".
            (And seen no more,
                After December 20, 1944.)

                                                    R.W. Abbott,
                                                        Author.

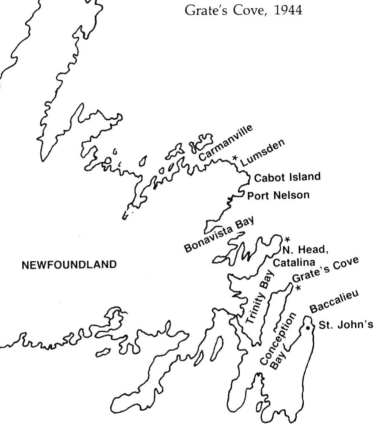

LOSS OF "ELLA M. RUDOLPH"

The ship's bell is sounded every half hour
Eight bells or sounds mark four o'clock
Eight o'clock and twelve o'clock.
(Mid-day and Midnight)

The "Ella M. Rudolph" strikes Northern Head.

'Ten minutes to eight'

The loss of
The Ella M. Rudolph
December 6, 1926

Author's Note

The public dispatch was in past years, written daily about noon by the Postmaster (who was also the telegraph operator) and put in the waiting room of the Post Office so the general public could see and read the news.

Those daily reports covered some foreign news, but the greater part consisted of local affairs, weather forecasts, shipping around the Newfoundland coast and more. Shipwrecks took priority over all other events, because they involved fishermen and lives of members of many families around the Island.

On December 7th, 1926, I read, "A schooner was lost last night at Northern Head near Little Catalina. Only one man saved."

This was also reported in **The Daily News**. We were very anxious to find out more details because Shipper Jesse West in the "Progress" from Carmanville was on his way down from St. John's the same day with winter supplies and men from Musgrave Harbour aboard. It was not the "Progress" as we found out soon after, but the schooner lost was the "Ella M. Rudolph" with all crew, except one, Duke Blackwood, who was miraculously washed up on a rocky ledge of a very steep cliff, and who later climbed to safety.

I wanted to write this story many times, but did not get down to doing so until 1974 when I had an occasion to visit my cousin, Duke's sister, at Little Catalina, and her husband, a Dalton, and relative of Mr. Levi Dalton with whom Duke stayed during his two days at Catalina after he was saved from the wrecked "Rudolph".

We went to Brook Cove, Northern Head and I saw the cliff which Duke climbed up that very stormy night. While we were at that scene I descended the cliff, almost to the ledge where Duke clung that night. I was able to take some pictures of it and the very high rugged cliff up which he climbed.

After returning from the Cove at Northern Head, I was able to gather much information from Mr. Dalton and some of the neighbours there who had seen Duke.

I wrote Duke at Dartmouth, N.S., where he resided with his daughter Joan, and told him how I had visited the place where he was shipwrecked, and told him I was ready to write the story if he would give me permission and all the information possible. He promised me he would visit Newfoundland in the summer and would call to see me about the subject.

He kept his promise and in 1975 we had a long chat together, and I was able to tape his story, from which I have been able to write his exact words.

I have written the story as it was related to me by Duke, and from my memory, using much of the sea language and dialect of our Newfoundland seamen which I believe is the way a story of this nature should be written. After examining all the evidence, it seems reasonably correct that the ledge described by Duke is where the "Ella M. Rudolph" went in broadside (as Duke says) when he jumped.

I am indebted not only to Duke, but also his sister, Mrs. Mary Dalton at Little Catalina, her husband who accompanied me to the scene at Brook Cove and Northern Head, Captain Theophilus W. Blackwood, who also remembers the tragedy very well. He commanded several schooners and owned the "Erma H." when she was wrecked at Lumsden, Newfoundland in 1929. I am also indebted to Mr. Reuben Vardy of Hickman's Harbour, whose brother James owned the "Rudolph" before he sold her to Eleazer Blackwood; and my mother who was able to give me the background of the Blackwood family tree. I also wish to thank Mr. N. Ray Wight of the Newfoundland Teachers' Association for his assistance. I took the title "Ten Minutes to Eight" from Duke's opening sentence in his narrative to me.

"I went below to the forecastle at ten minutes to eight to get a pair of dry warm mitts, it was my turn to take the wheel from the guy, and while I was there she struck."

The young man who in a moment of time decided to jump to safety, if possible, amid the darkness and roar of wind and sea, not knowing where he was but with hope and trust that he would land on safe ground and other souls do likewise ... I wanted more than ever to hear the full story from the lone survivor.

The "Ella M. Rudolph": A Description

The schooner "Ella M. Rudolph" was built at Allendale, Nova Scotia by Harold W. Allen, and registered at Shelbourne, N.S. in 1912. Her dimensions are given as 66.2 feet long: 18.9 feet wide; 8.2 feet deep and her gross tonnage as 53.95. She was very well built with a trim shape and a sailing bottom, a round bower for which those vessels were known and regarded as good sailers. Painted black with a yellow stripe about a foot below the top of the rail she carried two masts (or spars) with a bowspit. Fitted with mainsail, foresail, jumbo and jib, she also had a riding sail for lying-to in heavy wind or stormy weather. The main topmast helped to make her look graceful (as they used to say in those days). Many skipper men admired this type of schooner, dressed in their full suit of sails.

The "Ella M. Rudolph" was transferred to the Newfoundland Registry in 1915 when she was bought by Felix G. Tibbo of Grand Bank. Tibbo sold her to Charles R. Steer (he was one of the Steer Brothers on the waterfront of Water Street, St. John's) in 1918. In 1920 Steer sold her to Walter B. Spencer of Fortune. However, she was later sold to John Vardy and his war veteran son, James, after he returned home from the war in 1918. They resided at Hickman's Harbour, Trinity Bay, Newfoundland. They intended to use her for the Labrador fishery, however, the life or trade didn't seem to appeal to James and after a summer or two with little or no success, he decided to sell her.

Skipper Eleazer Blackwood saw the vessel was for sale and discussed the matter with his sons who agreed that it would be a fine schooner for them in the Labrador fishing trade. They purchased the "Rudolph" in the fall of 1925 and brought her home to Port Nelson, Bonavista Bay, Nfld., where she was laid up for that winter. In the spring she would be trimmed out for the fishing season, masts scraped down, new ropes attached to the sails, and the hull painted.

The Crew of the "Ella M. Rudolph"
December 6th, 1926

1. Skipper Eleazer Blackwood (father), Port Nelson, B.B. Nfld.
2. His sons: Bertram Blackwood, age 29 years (widower)
3.   Harry Blackwood, age 26 years (married two months)
4.   Duke Blackwood, age 20 years, single (survivor)
5. Crew members: Walter Attwood, age 31 years, married, Safe Harbour, B.B., Newfoundland
6.   Joseph Vivian, age 33 years, married, Hare Bay, Newfoundland
7.   Samuel Carter, age 52 years, married, Shambler's Cove, B.B., Newfoundland (An uncle of Duke)
8.   Noah Vivian, age 38 years, married, Shambler's Cove, B.B., Newfoundland
9. Cook: Mary Jane Abbott, single, Hare Bay, B.B., Newfoundland.

Duke was the only survivor. All the others were drowned and the bodies of five were recovered and buried; the skipper at Port Nelson, his home town; Mary Jane Abbott, at Hare Bay; Bertram and Harry Blackwood, Walter Attwood and Joseph Vivian were buried at Little Catalina. Samuel Carter and Noah Vivian were never recovered.

The Loss of "Ella M. Rudolph"

"I went below to the forecastle at ten minutes to eight to get a pair of dry warm mitts. It was my turn to take the wheel from the guy, and while I was in the forecastle she struck," so said Duke Blackwood, the sole survivor of the schooner "Ella M. Rudolph", which went down with seven men and one woman, after striking a rocky ledge on the cliffs of Northern Head near Catalina, Newfoundland on December 6, 1926.

As reported in **The Daily News** Wednesday, December 8, 1926:

"She must have went in broadside to the cliff, because she was broadside when I jumped. I jumped from the midship of the schooner over the side into the water. I didn't know where I was jumping.

"Then it all happened, and so suddenly," said Duke.

Like many others, the Blackwoods were seafearers who would just as soon be on the sea in a small boat as in a large schooner or steamer with little fear of stormy weather, high or smooth seas. They were born on or near the sea, and followed the waterway to earn their bread and butter. They aimed to have the best boats and put much of their earnings into the business, and became owners and masters of their vessels both at the fisheries and trading in local or foreign waters.

Our ancestors were hard workers, and determined to accomplish any task set them by way of earning a decent livelihood. Fishing of course was the main industry in our area, and most of those eager to do so settled as near the fishing grounds as possible, thus every island or cove that could be considered a suitable place to erect a wharf or fish stage and shelter a boat or schooner was regarded as a settlement, and homes were built with special attention given to the fishing premises.

Eleazer Blackwood and his family settled at Loo Cove (later Port Nelson), his father's home port as well.

Eleazer's family were Bertram, Harry and Duke, Carrie, Clara, Louise, Mary and Olive. Eleazer followed his father very closely by way of fishing at home and going to Labrador in his schooner of which he was master. When he became old enough and could arrange to get on his own he took charge and had a fishing crew of men including his own sons. He commanded the "H.F. Wilson", then the "Klondyke" "Sarah" and "Valiant", afterwhich he purchased the "Ella M. Rudolph" in 1925-26 from James Vardy of Hickman's Harbour, Newfoundland.

It would appear that Eleazer and his boys were proud of their schooner because it is said they maintained her well. This of course was necessary, it was their second home and had to be kept as such; using it on the Labrador in the summer to live in; storing the fish they caught to be brought home in late August or early September and cured, sold and from the returns purchase the winter's food and supplies required to get them started off again on the next summer's voyage.

To Labrador Fishing

It was in this lovely schooner that skipper Eleazor and crew went to Labrador in the summer of 1926 to try his luck (as they say) at getting a sapper. That is, a full load of fish.

They usually start sometime in May to get ready. The traps, lines and twines are all prepared in later winter in the twine loft on the premises. Then as soon as possible the schooner is made seaworthy by heaving her down, caulking the necessary plank seams, coppering the bottom, painting the hull outside, scraping down the spars, painting the booms, cabin and wheel house, the deck, then the living quarters, the forecastle and cabin below. Now to bend on the canvas, that is attach it securely to the booms, spars and bend the halyards and sheets, hoist it all for a close inspection and proud satisfaction concluded with "Boy, she's a dandy!"

As soon as one fishing season closed, another one began. The settling up and conclusion of work ended about mid December, then a few days of rest and taking stock of the past year's activities and earning, etc., errors and mistakes adjusted and used for stepping stones for the future. The skipper would begin to get restless and wanted to get going again. If they didn't go to the seal fishery, as many of them did, then it was time to get at the nets and cod traps. Thus many hours were spent on the twine loft; where much discussion as well as work took place and sometimes decisions were made in advance, as to how, when and where the voyage to Labrador would take place.

With most of winter gone and spring advancing it was time to walk out on the frozen harbour to check the condition of the good old schooner inside and out as far as could be seen above water. Later the whole of the vessel would be looked over, and in time made ready for the summer's fishing trip to Labrador.

Then one good day in late May a fair wind and the weather glass (barometer) showing the same for a while, the crew was called on board, the mainsail hoisted, the anchors weighed and the "Rudolph" like other schooners headed for St. John's to fit out with supplies and provisions for the Labrador fishing season.

Duke Blackwood says, "That year, meaning 1926, we started around the middle of May and later went to St. John's to get our provisions for the summer."

"Then we came home and barked our traps and got everything ready to go to the Labrador. That year I think we were ready and sailed about the first or second week in June. There was some ice around and we had to work our way down. We had no power, only the sails, so we had to go by the winds, go in harbour when necessary and out again next day or as soon as possible and work our way down the coast. That year we went as far as Cape Harrison. My father knew about the traps berths there and so he thought it might be a good place to get our fish. There were several other schooners there and we finished up there with, I think, somewhere around six hundred quintals (112 lbs. dried or cured fish), then we bore-up for home. We got home sometime in late August or early September and after a short while father decided to take out the fish and try to get it made and carry it to St. John's for shipment, then get our winter's supplies and return home. We planned to go into the bay for a load of firewood to bring home for the winter, that was his plans, but it never happened," said Duke.

The Trip to St. John's

Duke said, "I remember that fall was not a good fish making year, and we were late before we had ours all made ready for shipping. However, in October we managed to get underway and left Port Nelson with a light north west wind which was in our favour to St. John's which we reached the next day, just afternoon, and anchored in the stream (as St. John's Harbour was often called by the fishermen in schooners).

Before we left home it was our intention to just have the summer crew only, but mother thought she'd like to go along as well to help dad get some of the winter's supplies, and she did, leaving my youngest sister at home with Grandmother Blackwood, so our house was closed up while we were away.

On our arrival at St. John's father and Bert went ashore to try and sell our fish. They had some difficulty in doing so because of so much sold that year and the markets well stocked. However, we were successful after a long time in persuading Monroe's to purchase our cargo and we pulled in next day to the pier and started to unload. The weather was not the best and it took some time before we finished. After a few days when everyone had purchased what they could for the winter, the "Rudolph" was loaded and the hatches battened down and we were ready to sail for home. The weather was very stormy all the fall, but it was getting worst now in December with high westerly and north westerly winds and several snow flurries. Most of the schooners had gone earlier, except for a few from Conception or Trinity Bays and the southern shore which might make it in a day or two homeward.

We waited around, tied up to the wharf, hoping for a south or southwest wind to get a quick run down the shore and home. At night someone of the crew would go up to the Post Office, and read the latest or midnight weather forecast and wind directions for the next day or two, and if favourable, get a short nap of sleep and try to get underway as early as possible in the morning even before daybreak try to clear The Narrows, and head north toward Cape St. Francis. This was the usual custom of all the skipper men in the sailing vessels. I remember it well," said Duke. "We were all very happy and longing to get out of St. John's and home. My mother and sister decided after a while to come home by train to Port Blandford and by the "S.S. Malokoff" from there to Greenspond. Since it was rather late in the fall to be on a sailing craft (schooners were often called crafts), that's what she did and of course she was not in the tragedy."

Homeward Bound

The 6th day of December, 1926, Duke said, "we left St. John's around 9:00 o'clock we squared away outside The Narrows about an hour afterwards and such a beautiful day the sun was shining, a light breeze from the south and she was making fair time. Everything looked alright and we were happy. After we straightened away, the cook prepared the dinner and all except the men at the wheel went below for the nice flavoured food of meat and vegetables. The girl, Mary Jane Abbott, was given her's in the cabin, where she was resting in the bunk because one of the men was doing a bit of cooking that day. All hands came down in the forecastle and sat around the table as we did many a time that summer, and the usual conversations took place about the past summer, the trap berths, next summer, if God spares us, we'll try for that other berth and so on. What we plan for next winter and, the price of fish and food now. 'There's a good many dollars worth in this one now,' said one of the crew. 'Yes', said another. 'I'd like to have the worth of her', and so the conversations went, and dinner was finished and dishes cleared away. Some of the men jumped up in their bunks for a short nap before their watch came on; while the regular watch went on deck. Father went aft to the cabin and tapped the glass (barometer). Someone said, 'The wind is freshening up skipper'. 'Yes, the glass is going down. Three tenths since this morning we came out.' 'How's the wind?' 'Tis southerly and backing our easterly, yes, it'll be southeast afore dark.' 'What time is it boys?' father asked. 'Around 12 o'clock, sir. We should be through Baccalieu tickle by two or three o'clock. If the wind increases we'll make Catalina by stone dark anyway and harbour for the night.'

Meanwhile one and another was going up and down the forecastle to get a warm cup of tea or see how everything was going. It was getting cold and chilly, and the sky was overcast. Father checked the glass again, 'Still going down boys. You know that wind is piping up fast.' 'That's snow I believe skipper,' said one of the crew. 'What time is it?' 'About four o'clock skipper.' 'Yes, we should pass the tickle (Baccalieu Tickle) about another hour I suppose. If we had wind like this the morning, we'd been well over to Catalina now.'

'The glass is still going, almost to twenty-nine. After we get through boys, all hands will have to come on deck and keep a good watch out for Green Island light or the sound of the horn. It's getting dark early now, it's thick too. All hands on deck, except for a man or two would go down below to keep the fire going or to get on his oil skins and a dry pair of mitts. We could see now that father was getting anxious as we all were. It was really blowing a storm and wet blinding snow as thick as it could be, it was dark. The starboard and port sidelights were up and the light in the binnacle. Father set the course for Catalina, and told the man at the wheel to try and keep her dead on course, for we want to make Catalina if possible. She was running wild and the waves breaking fore and aft. It looked as if we were in for a bad night if we didn't reach Green Island and see the light or hear the horn and get our bearing for the harbour. Father said, 'Boys, we'll heave too and reef the mainsail and foresail.' It was a terrible time in the dark trying to get the canvas down, in the wind, sea, and snow. You just had to hold unto whatever you could and try as hard as you could to tie down the works. Sometimes you had to let go and grab for whatever you thought was safe, because the schooner was rolling and up and down in the heavy waves, and the sleety snow made it slippery and dangerous on deck. Finally, we managed to get it tied up a bit and we got the reefed mainsail and jumbo on her again and she steadied a bit. Then father decided to change the course from north to northeast.

He said, 'we'll never make in on Catalina shores like this, so we'll haul her out northeast and try to get around Bonavista Cape outside of the old Harry's and by daylight we'll be in Bonavista Bay. The wind might slack then and we can run for Port Nelson or up in the bay somewhere. Let's get the riding-sail on her now, boys. All hands hold on and be careful what you're doing. Watch her at the wheel." Duke says: "It was a blizzard, blowing a storm. We tried three times to get the riding sail on her and every time the hook came unhooked the sail went wild in the wind. We had to stand clear and let it down as quick as possible, and try to tie it down. Father said, 'We'll have to give it up boys, it's too bad on deck and not much we can do only watch out all you can. It'll be better after twelve, always a change then better or worse. It can't get much worse though. What time is it now boys?' father said. He spoke to one or two of the crew nearest him. 'I suppose it's nearly eight o'clock now, we spent a good spell at that riding-sail. Too bad we couldn't get it on her, she'd been much steadier.' ' 'Tis pretty rough now skipper,' said one man. My brother Bert was standing aloneside of Father, just forward of the mainmast on the portside. 'Duke', he said, 'you'll have to take the wheel now and relieve Noah. 'Tis nearly eight o'clock, my she's tumbling about shockin', what a night! A storm of wind and a blizzard of snow from the southeast, once she gets around the Cape there won't be as much lumper and she'll be steadier, I hope.' Duke says: "I then went below at ten minutes to eight. It was my turn to take the wheel from the guy. I went down the forecastle to get a dry pair of mitts. The lamp was lit on the pawpost, and a little fire in the stove. I thought I would put in a junk or two to keep it warm for the boys coming off watch. Walter Attwood was there, he was getting ready to go on deck too. I had no sooner decided to get my mitts and was reaching for them when I heard the bang right on the portside and everything went in a terrible tremble. I rushed for the companionway, and up the ladder, in the dim light of the forecastle I could just see Walter's long rubber rushing up the last step or two of the ladder. He went somewhere on deck, I don't know where, I never saw him again. I rushed aft and was right by Bert's right shoulder while father was shouting, 'Call the girl, we're ashore on Northern Head or somewhere here.' At the same time, neither Bert nor I uttered one word that I can remember, as I know of, and I couldn't see father. I caught the glimpse of Bert jump up on the rail and overboard. I followed immediately. Bert must have went under the side of the schooner when the sea washed out. I never saw him after. I jumped on what seemed a little bench of rock and got washed in against what looked like a sharp rock sticking up above the rest; and which I graped with my both arms and held on, but when the sea went it it tore my left arm away from the rocks, and I lost my mitt, but I managed to hold on with my right arm which sort of jammed in the crevase, and as soon as the sea was gone out enough I made a dash for the higher rocks which the next sea only lifted me up a bit, and I continued to climb up over the ledge of the cliff, waist deep in snow and soaking wet from head to foot in my oil skins. I kept on climbing with the snow and wind in my back forcing me against the huge cliff of rocks until sometime later, I don't know exactly how long, I reached the top and climbed in over. I sort of felt I was up over the worst of the cliff because the wind was higher, and I began to move down toward a valley-like decline."

The author said to him, "Did you look back after you got so far up the cliff to see if you could see anything or hear anyone call out?"

"No," said Duke, "I couldn't look back or down the cliff. It was too stormy and blinding snow, and all I could hear all the way up the cliff was the roar of wind and sea. There was nothing I could see; it was all over in the matter of seconds and the schooner was gone to matchwood."

He said, "She must have gone in broadside to the cliff on the portside, because I jumped from the midship unto the rocks when the sea went out. Bert jumped when she struck, apparently on the same sea that washed her in there. I don;t know where the other men were, aft or foreward at the time they could have been looking out one place or the other. The girl was in the bunk in the cabin. That's why father called out to someone who he thought was near the cabin or wheel: to call the girl. We might be able to get ashore perhaps, but there was no chance. Apparently the following seas must have swept over the starboard side, and washed everyone overboard or they might have been hit with the booms or blocks or tangled in some ropes. No one knows or ever will, I suppose.

I think the lights were up as far as I know. They were up all night anyway, and the jumbo and foresail was on her, but no doubt everything gave way in a short time. Nothing came across me in the ways of wreckage, and apparently she drifted back in a little gulch and broke up; that's where her anchors and chains were while other parts of the wreckage drifted up a little cove called Brook Cove. That's where they found the girl on a little sand beach. The only place there like that. They had to lower men down the cliffs by ropes to get her."

"After I got to the top of the cliff," said Duke, "I walked inward as I thought with my back still to the wind until I came to a little valley and a little thicket of woods. I was lost for a while not knowing where I was in the dark with snow waist deep. I decided to stay there a while, which I did, walking around and around trying to keep warm until I could decide what to do next. Meanwhile, the snow stopped about 2:30 a.m. and it became a little lighter. I could see around me and I decided to move out of the woods and climbed a little hill like, I saw a light.

Father said we were ashore on Northern Head. I figured it must be towards Catalina, so I started travelling over the hills and marshes, through the snow and across the bottom of a small pond which they told me after was Brook Cove Pond and on until I came to a garden fence. I could see the lights in Port Union. I passed by a barn or store then I came out on the road. There was a rail on the outside of the road so I guided myself along by it and fell down where I tried to regain my strength. I leaned across the rail for about ten or fifteen minutes perhaps and accidently turned to look around over my right shoulder and saw a light upstairs in a house just across the road. I crawled over on my hands and knees and tried to knock on the front door, but nobody seemed to hear me. It was blowing and I was very cold. I crawled around then to the back door and knocked again. After a few minutes or so someone (Mr. Levi Dalton) called out and said, "Who's there?" I was too weak to answer and I didn't know what to say so he quietly opened the door and I said, "A schooner lost and all hands at Northern Head, I suppose, and I got washed ashore."

At Levi Dalton's, Catalina

I was completely exhausted and couldn't say anymore at the time. Mr. Dalton helped me into the porch and in the kitchen and I sat down, hungry, tired, soaking wet, and cold. In a very short while Mrs. Dalton was up and they lit the fire in the kitchen stove, boiled the kettle and by the time they had my oil skins, long rubbers which were full of water, and wet cloths off, a cup of warm tea was ready for me as well as some brandy and spirits to revive me. I began to feel a little better and soon they had me put to bed, wrapped in warm blankets, and I soon fell asleep. I couldn't talk much. I could only tell them enough to inform them where I thought the wreck was and about what time it happened, and how I made my way to Catalina. They understood my sad plight and circumstances and were most anxious to get me well enough to give them more information later. I was so exhausted and tired that I must have slept very soundly until the evening when I awoke. They had already called the doctor and as soon as I was able to answer his questions he gave me a complete check-up and found me recovering very well after the terrible ordeal. He said I was very good, but needed a day or two complete rest and relaxing. I stayed with Mr. and Mrs. Dalton for two days. They were very good to me and watched me with intensive care and followed the doctor's orders. After two days I was able to go to Big Catalina to stay with my aunt for a day or two, my father's sister Aunt Louise Carter, before I got ready to go home. I had to get clothes before I could make the trip home, which was provided for me by the people there, all of whom were very kind to help me in any way possible.

Meanwhile, at Mr. and Mrs. Dalton's, things were moving fast. Mrs. Dalton was preparing a meal for me, and got the bed warm and ready, while Mr. Dalton lost no time in calling up the neighbours and briefly relating the story to them. Soon lights were going in all over the towns and men were ready to start immediately with lanterns, ropes and gafts, luncheons, warm clothing, and everything they thought would be required to rescue any survivors who might be in the cliff or around Brook Cove Beach. It was not long before they were on their way to Brook Cove and Northern Head to where I informed them that I believe the wreck was. They knew the shorter route and soon arrived on the scene, but since it was not quite light, nothing was visible and they could only hear the roar of the sea and heavy gale of wind. However, when daylight broke they were horrified to see nothing only broken timber and wreckage thrown along the bottom of the cliff and up as far as Brook Cove where much of the cargo and parts of the vessel had drifted. They then went to the place where they thought the "Rudolph" struck and lowered men by ropes down over the cliffs to see if there were any survivors who could not get up the cliff on their own or had washed ashore in the crevase of the rocks or tangled in the wreckage but there was not a trace of anyone or anything. They noticed the place where Duke climbed up and wondered how he ever did it without help. But someone unseen helped him," said Duke. "They then traced along the cliff the best way they could but due to the heavy sea and strong winds not much could be done. However, on coming to Brook Cove where there happened to be a little sandy beach they lowered down some more men, and they noticed something on the crest of a wave which happened to be a body floating towards the beach. It was that of the girl, Mary Jane Abbott, which they prepared and had her pulled up the cliff and brought to Catalina ready for burial in Hare Bay. They were hoping to find others among the wreckage but it was too rough to get out very far. Meanwhile, those people never stopped hunting around and on the lookout until all the bodies were recovered except two. They were Samuel Carter, age 52 years, husband of Clara, and Noah Vivian, 38 years old of Shambler's Cove, and one of the summer crew. Eleazer Blackwood, skipper, was recovered sometime after the others and buried at Port Nelson, while the two sons, Bert and Harry, along with Walter Attwood and Joseph Vivian, were buried at Catalina.

 The news soon spread around Catalina and Port Union as well as by telegraph around the island as reported in **The Daily News**, December 8, 1926 and men came from everywhere in the area to assist and help in any way they could to get the bodies of the drowned crew. As soon as Duke's Uncle Edward, who lived in Trinity then heard of it, he went down to supervise the search and make burial arrangements. He stayed down a week or more and when it was suitable they went out in motorboats to see if anything else could be found or salvages that might be of assistance in recovering the two missing bodies, but after a long while and with the very stormy weather on, they had to give up; although men often kept an eye out to see if any trace of the bodies might be found. Even during the following summer a watch out was conducted once in a while for any new trace of recovery. The anchors and chains were found very close to where it was believed the "Rudolph" struck the cliff and Duke jumped overboard, proving that she must have beaten up almost instantly in the terrible gale and sea.

Duke said earlier that his mother decided to go home by train instead of on the "Rudolph". Since it was late in the season, she wanted to see her daughter on the way home, at Port Blandford then join the "S.S. Malokoff" for Greenspond where her brother lived, then from Greenspond across the tickle to Port Nelson their home. By the time she'd got home in the "Rudolph" she'd be home at the same time. That was the plan, but alas! it did not materialize, tragedy intervened and the stormy seas engulfed the ship and crew.

Meanwhile, there was very little Duke could do at Catalina. He decided to go home to Port Nelson, and meet his mother and relatives. So he boarded the train for Gambo, then take passage on one of the small boats going down the bay as far as Wesleyville, landing of course at Greenspond, where he would meet his mother, who had already arrived there by the "S.S. Malokoff" and while everyone knew of the tragedy on the boat, nobody had informed Mrs. Blackwood, or as they say "broke the news to her" until the Minister called to see at Greenspond.

"The meeting was a very sad one, only a couple of members of the large family left, then they returned to Loo Cove and stayed with Grandfather Blackwood", said Duke, and after a few days went back into their own house for the winter. A lonely spot but trying to make the best of it. It was not a happy Christmas," said Duke. However, time is a great healer and seasons rolled around. Duke stayed at home that summer, but later went to Buchans where he obtained a job to earn money to provide for the family. "And things would right itself again," said Duke.

Meanwhile Duke went back to Catalina in the spring and they took him out in boat to the scene of the tragedy to see the ledge on which he believes he jumped that stormy night from the rail of the "Rudolph". Some years after he went to sea again with his uncle, but soon returned to land and on to Toronto for twenty-three years. However, now he resides in Dartmouth, N.S.

Duke, during the interview often broke the line of the story to inject some kind remarks for the people of Catalina who did such services in rendering every effor to recover the bodies of the crew lost in the tragedy. They kept up their vigilant search to the very last that winter, and renewed the same in the spring and summer for the two who were still in the sea, but never recovered after that terrible southeast gale of high wind, snow and rough sea on the rugged shore of high cliffs and treacherous shoals near Northern Head, Trinity Bay, Newfoundland, at "Ten Minutes to Eight".

It all happened so suddenly in a matter of seconds. "She must have gone in broadside," said Duke, about "ten minutes to eight".

The Song
Loss of the "Ella M. Rudolph"
(by Hughie Sexton, Trinity, T.B., December, 1926)

Attention all ye fishermen, and toilers of the sea,
While I relate these lines to you, of an awful tragedy,
Which leaves so many families in sorrow to bewail
For the loss of sons and husbands, caused by that dreadful gale.

The "Ella M. Rudolph" a vessel staunch, and a clever sea boat too,
Her Skipper's name was Blackwood, and eight composed her crew;
A female also was on board, then so gayly and bright,
She with the rest did meet her doom, on that sad fatal night.

On the sixth day of December the Rudolph left the town
Full load of general cargo, for Port Nelson she was bound;
With a gentle breeze of south west wind, the schooner sailed along,
But the sky was thick and heavy, and night was coming on.

At five o'clock that evening, through the "tickle" she did pass,
When threatenings of a violent storm was showing by the glass;
When from South-East the wind did veer, with storms all through the night,
The Skipper's intention was to try and make Catalina light.

Not very far out in the bay the schr. she did reach,
When the Skipper changed his course again from North unto North-East,
Thinking the ship would round the cape and reach Bonavista Bay,
But under her foresail and jumbo, unfortunately made lee way.

Eight fine strong men, that very night, upon her deck did stand,
With eager minds and piercing eyes all on the look out for land,
When the wind blew strong, and the seas ran high, Oh! what a terrible plight,
When the "Ella M. Rudolph" end her days, on Catalina shore that night.

The vessel scarcely struck the rocks before covered with the waves,
All of her crew except one man did meet a watery grave;
This poor young chap jumped overboard 'mid blinding snow and drift,
And by the guiding hand of Providence was hurled in the cliff.

He wend his way all up the cliff, through blinding sleet and snow,
O'er marshes, fields and valleys, not knowing where to go
To look for hospitalities and comfort for the night,
When to his surprise, before his eyes, saw Little Catalina lights.

It was early next morning, about the hour of four,
After eight long hours of travelling he reached Levi Dalton's door
Who kindly answered to his knock and a saddening sight did see,
A lad standing there with oilskins on, a miracle from the sea.

Come in my lad, come in, this man did kindly say,
And tell me what has happened and how you came this way;
This boy was so exhausted and all that he did say
A schooner lost, and all her crew not very far away.

Now with this kindly woman the poor lad did reside
And with hot drinks, and clothing warm, she soon did him revive,
Which after rest and medical aid, the tale he told anew
The sorrowful fate of the "Rudolph" and the loss of all her crew.

This man soon told his neighbours, and soon the news were spread,
And men before so very long, were raising from their bed,
With ropes and gaffs and lanterns too, one night so dark and drear,
The path was thronged with men, from Brook Cove they did steer.

At last they arrived upon the scene, but sadly heard no sound,
They searched with vain endeavours, but no creature could be found,
But when the dawning broke again such an awful sight to see,
A schooner's wreckage washed ashore, while her crew were in the sea.

These willing men did try their might some bodies for to get,
But the sea was raging furiously and dashing by the cliff,
But an awful sight came before their eyes as they stood there next day,
To see a body wash ashore upon a heaving wave.

This chanced to be the female once so gay with game
An Abbott girl from Hare Bay, her name was Mary Jane.
And soon with kind and willing hands, her body did prepare,
And sent along for Burial Rights, to her mother's home so dear.

Not one day had passed away but these men were on the spot,
And after days of toiling five bodies more they got;
And now they are resting in their graves beneath the church yard sod,
But their souls have fled to its place of rest, in the Paradise of God.

So now my friends and comrades, there's one thing more to do:
Let us not forget the widows, and the little orphans too,
Whom through this great disaster are left fatherless in their homes,
But the Lord knows what is best, and His will must be done.

Now in conclusion let us not forget our friends,
The people of Catalina who worked with willing hands
For to recover those bodies their labour did not spare
May a blessing rest on Catalina, and all its citizens there.

But two more bodies still are lying beneath the ocean waves,
Waiting for their Saviour's call on the last Great Judgement Day,
When the sea it will give up its dead, as told by Scripture true,
May the Lord have mercy on the souls of the "Ella M. Rudolph's" crew.

The lone survivor, Duke Blackwood, one year later at age 21.

Levi Dalton of Little Catalina

The jagged rocks near where the Ella M. Rudolph was lost and where Duke Blackwood jumped ashore X

Levi Dalton's house showing the front door where Duke Blackwood first knocked before going to the back on hands and knees, in an exhausted condition.

Duke Blackwood in 1974. He is seated on the rock in Port Nelson where his family home once stood.

'She's gone adrift, boys'

The loss of
The Erema H.
1929

I dedicate this story of my trip, to my mother, Dorcas (Blackwood) Abbott, and in remembrance of my late father, George D. Abbott for their continued devotion in prayer for our safe return during the whole voyage.

and;

Also, present it to Mr. Theophilus William Blackwood, the skipper of the "Erema H." for his sincere care, and skill as a good skipper and seaman. He was only a young man at the time, but displayed the courage and keen judgement of a fully qualified sea captain.

The Loss of the Erema H. 1929

The "Erema H." was a schooner of 71 tons 30 tenths, oak built and copper fastened, built at La Have, N.S. She was lost about 6:30 a.m., December 2nd., 1929 when she parted her main chain, and shortly afterwards the second chain broke allowing her to drift leeward unto South Cat Harbour Island, Lumsden, Newfoundland.

I relate this story as it applies to me, and the crew involved while on the trip from the time we left home at Musgrave Harbour, Nfld. until we landed on the beach at Lumsden and I rode home on horse and sleigh.

It was my second trip to St. John's, the capital of Newfoundland. I had visited there once before with my father when I was younger, but this time I was on my own; except in the care of my uncle, Mr. Theophilus William Blackwood. He was my mother's brother, and was always called "son". Uncle Son to all of us.

This voyage was to be the last one for the season. I was anxious to get an eye examination and glasses because it was difficult for me to do much study at school without the aid of glasses; especially in front of a kerosene lamp light. We had no electricity in those days. I planned to further my education during the coming winter, and do what I could with a navigation course at home, private and by correspondence.

It was October 21st., 1929, that the "Erema H." happened to be landing freight at Musgrave Harbour for fishermen who had gone to St. John's with their summer's catch to sell and buy their winter's food supplies. Now they were landing it from the schooner in motor boats.

I left our house and walked all the way up to the Harbour where some of the men were landing their supplies, and when the motor boat went out again to the "Erema" I went out to see uncle Son, and ask him if I could go to St. John's with him during the next trip. I said father is already up there now and I could see him before returning home.

"Alright," he said, "Come on aboard, we are leaving here as soon as the last item of freight is out for home at Carmanville. Tomorrow we're going to Gander Bay and land some more freight there."

I came ashore, walked down to our house, quickly packed my suitcase and took off with my oil clothes under my arm, and hurried up to the schooner just in time to catch the last boat out to the "Erema" for the last load of freight. I was happy to speak to uncle Son and step on the deck for what I thought would be only a few days of good sailing and an enjoyable trip to St. John's.

We hoisted the sails and steered for Carmanville. Skipper Stephen Goodyear in the "Undine" was still landing freight at Musgrave Harbour. Meanwhile, we had a few packages of freight for Mr. Jacob Pinsent, Merchant at Ladle Cove; which we intended to land on the way to Carmanville. However, just after we left Musgrave Harbour the wind died down until it was dead calm, and Uncle Stephen and Pierce Blackwood got out in the motor boat which we had in tow and carried the freight ashore.

They did not delay very long, just long enough to land the items and off again to join the schooner for Carmanville. The wind came up again from the south, a fine breeze and we soon reached the home port.

Our crew were: Theophilus Blackwood, Skipper and owner of the "Erema", Stephen Blackwood, mate, Charles E. Blackwood; three brothers and my uncles. Pierce Blackwood, my cousin and Edward Ellsworth all from Carmanville. I was a passenger, but on as one of the crew to do whatever I was asked and help handle the cargo from time to time, at least keep the kettle boiled for Pierce, the cook.

When we got to Carmanville, some of the other passengers who had been visiting relatives at Musgrave Harbour were put on board the small motor boat and carried ashore, as they all belonged to Carmanville.

Freight for Gander Bay

The crew returned to the schooner just after day break, and we set sail for Gander Bay to land freight at Clarke's Head for Mr. Frank Saunders, General Merchant. I remember some of it was "tins" for canning rabbits which would be caught during the winter.

It was a fine day and we went up to the reach of the bay with the booms all cross, with the main boom on the port side. Since the days were shortening, it was near dark before we arrived. so we dropped anchor and decided to stay all night and land the freight in the morning.

I had never been at Clarke's Head before, and I was surprised at the force of the tide coming out of the Gander Bay River; it kept us stern to the wind blowing up the bay nearly all night. However, in the morning we landed Mr. Saunder's freight in the small boat, and immediately steered for our home port, Carmanville. On our way down from Gander Bay I saw the wrecked steamship "Dundee" ashore on Grassy Island since the night of December 25th., 1919. She could not be refloated due to heavy slob ice at that time of the year. I recall hearing my father talking about her when she was lost. We got back to Carmanville late in the evening and dropped our anchor. It was October 23rd., 1929. And now we were ready to begin loading lumber at Mr. Willis Tulk's premises to be taken to Bay Roberts, Nfld.

Loading Lumber and Away

It was October 24th., Thursday morning when we began to take on the lumber at Mr. Tulk's, bringing it off the wharf unto the schooner and stowing it in the hold, using every available space to pack in all we could before taking on the deck load.

Right from the beginning the weather was very stormy with wet sleety snow now and then; which caused much delay in getting the board stowed and put on deck. We did not finish until the following Wednesday, October 30th., 1929.

Our load was assigned to another lumber dealer, a Mr. Bishop at Bay Roberts, Conception Bay, Nfld.

However, as they used to say then, "If you wait for a time along, you will surely get it" and our turn came with a fine morning on Thursday, October the 31st., the last day of the month when we weighed anchor about nine o'clock and sailed out of Carmanville Harbour bound south with a good time all down the "Straight Shore" with the booms across her, never thinking that she may not return that way again.

We sailed all day with a beautiful time along, and reached well across Bonavista Bay, until we saw the light on Bonavista Cape. Then I decided to go off watch and turn in the bunk for the night. It was nearly calm all night; just enough wind to keep her under steerage way, as they used to say when it was calm and only sails used. We sailed all night and all the next day, November 1st. until we reached Baccalieu Tickle and were well up towards Bay de Verde Head, when it got dead calm and the sails flopped about uselessly. The skipper then decided to get out our small motor boat and tow the schooner for awhile, making slow progress, but yet we accomplished three or four miles up the bay, until the wind sprang up and we began to beat tack upon tack all night until we reached Bay Roberts the next day about four o'clock in the afternoon, Saturday, November 2nd., 1929. Next day, Sunday, we, Pierce Blackwood and I, went ashore in the evening to stroll around, but we afterwards decided to go to The Salvation Army for an hour or more before going aboard for the night.

Bay Roberts and St. John's

Very few skipper men would work or sail on Sunday; except in the case of an emergency, and our skipper was one of them. However, Monday began fair and fine, so we began to unload our cargo of lumber and it was close to nightfall when we finished next day, Tuesday, November 5th., Bonfire Night. Wednesday, it was very stormy and we had to stay tied up to the pier until Thursday morning when we got underway and left for St. John's in company with the schooner "James Strong" a 140 ton vessel commanded by Skipper Wiseman from Little Bay Islands, Green Bay. We both arrived at St. John's entering The Narrows (The Harbour) about one o'clock in the afternoon. It blew a light breeze all day, and several schooners left St. John's in the morning but had only reached Cape St. Francis around the noon hour after beating down the shore going north. We knew at least two or three of them. The "Tritonia" Skipper E. Collins, and the "D.M. Hilton" Skipper John Goodyear both from Carmanville. My father was on the "Hilton" with other fishermen from my home who went to St. John's that fall with their fish for sale and to buy their winter's supplies.

Now they were on their way home.

We passed so close to them that Uncle Charles and my cousin Pierce lifted me up bodily to let my father know I was on board and bound for St. John's. He was standing by the wheel and signalled back by waving both arms.

We arrived at St. John's, as I mentioned before, and tied up at Baine Johnston Ltd. wharf where we discharged eighty-two and half quintals of dried fish which we had on board for some fishermen from Carmanville. It fetched $10.50 per quintal on an average, but just after that the price went down to around $3.25 per quintal. It was the year when the Great Depression began, and fishermen as well as all other labourers in the country faced the great decline in work. The economy was at a very low ebb.

St. John's

Just after we finished taking out the fish and began to clear away, we noticed several people coming down the wharf in a hurry including a policeman. Some of our men jumped upon the wharf to find out what was going on around the center of the wharf. After a few minutes we found that one of the employees at Baine Johnston Ltd. had suffered a severe heart attack and died quite suddenly.

Also tied up to the wharf close to us was Skipper William Collins of the "Helen Vair" who was taking on freight for Northern Ports. On Monday, November 11th. we pulled out from the wharf and sailed up the Harbour to tie up at Steers Ltd., where we had freight ready to take on board. We could not work or load very quickly because nearly every day was stormy with snow and a gale of westerly wind.

Captain William Collins came on board for a chat nearly every evening after he was ready to go and waiting for a time to get out. He told skipper he had bought a beautiful horse today and was taking it down to Carmanville. On Thursday he had a new jumbo (jib) bended on (that is, attached to the jumbo boom). We went down to see the horse and help load it on the deck of the schooner which was still at Baine Johnston's wharf. It was a lovely animal, chestnut red and looked so smart.

The "Helen Vair" left next morning, Friday, November 15th., for home; all very happy with their full load of freight and the noble animal to show one and all at Carmanville.

With the wind as it was at the time and the weather forecasted for the next day or so, they should reach Carmanville by the end of the week, and go on north to finish discharging the cargo then home to tie up for the winter and lay off the crew.

The Loss of the "Helen Vair"

However, such was not their fortune, and they did not see Carmanville again until mid January; the horse was buried at sea and the schooner sank.

The "Helen Vair", after leaving St. John's, sailed all day and night until Saturday afternoon when she arrived off the reef known as Edward's Reef about one and a half miles off Musgrave Harbour, and not much more than an hour or two from Carmanville, the home port.

But, alas! It was a stormy evening with the wind blowing almost a hurricane down the Bay. With a tight sheet and battened down, the schooner ran into a heavy gust of wind, 'a feather white ocean' and sea, and with spray covering the "Helen" from stem to stern and half way up the spars, the canvas tore away from the spars and booms in pieces and blew overboard. The main top-end lift broke and the boom came down. In a few moments every thing was in a confusion. Theodore Ellsworth was at the wheel and suffered a broken arm when the main boom came down across the cabin and wheel.

There seemed to be only one course to take, to square away to the open sea for the night. It was a long cold bitter night. For several days the "Helen" drifted away out to sea eventually reaching some 450 miles off Cape Spear, Nfld. she was later sighted by the S.S. Terne which steamer took the crew onboard just before the "Helen" became waterlogged and sank. They were obliged to sail with the steamer to Carthagena, Spain. The crew of eight men did not get home before January 1930.

We knew the storm came up and wondered if Skipper Collins reached home.

It was Monday, November 18th. about 4:30 p.m. I was in the forecastle of our schooner with all our crew reading the Evening Telegram and the brief news about the "Helen Vair" being driven off in Saturday's hurricane which struck her just off Musgrave Harbour, and was driven off seaward and there was no further news of her.

While I was reading the news of the "Helen Vair", with the crew listening in silence, our schooner began to vibrate and tremble.

The skipper, being annoyed, thinking that someone was shaking the shrouds or on the bowsprite or jib boom, sent uncle Charlie up to investigate the cause.

Charlie came back to say that there was no one up there. The schooner shook again, and we were all surprised and began to look around to locate the strange noise. We did not find out anything to cause the vibration. Later in the evening we learned that an earthquake had occurred, and a tidal wave had swept the south coast of Newfoundland and caused damage and loss of life especially at Burin and surrounding communities. Our schooner shortly after rose well up above the wharf with the unusually high tide. The quake was felt all over Newfoundland.

It was a very stormy fall, and we were still in St. John's, for a long time loaded and waiting several days for a favourable time to go home.

I enjoyed the city, and going around the different streets looking at the displays of goods in the store windows, visiting the different schooners tied up and waiting for a time out and a fair wind home.

I went to a Mr. C.D. Slater on Water Street West and he gave me an eye test and fitted me with glasses with large black frames which cost at that time the sum of $8.00 which I thought was enough since the test only took about a few minutes. Not more than a half hour from the time I left the schooner had passed before I was back again with all the crew taking stock of me and examining my spectacles, and trying them on one after the other.

We walked up and down the streets, mostly Water Street, down on the wharves chatting with the skippers and crew of the several schooners waiting as we were; just before midnight we would go up to the Post Office and read the latest weather report.

Bound For Home

I was happy on Thursday morning when the skipper called us to hoist the sails and get underway for home. It was midday before we were out clear and sailing down St. John's Harbour and on down the shore in company with the "Undine" (Skipper Stephen Goodyear), the "Catherine P." (Skipper Timothy Collins) and several other schooners going north.

As we sailed along and down towards Cape St. Francis the light winds of early morning began to increase as the day shortened, until it blew a gale from the west north west. It was too much for the "Catherine P." and Skipper Collins decided to return home on the "S.S. Home" the Coastal Mail Boat, on the St. John's-Change Islands run. That ended his trips for the season.

The "Erema H." and "Undine" (Skipper Stephen Goodyear) and two other schooners came on across Conception Bay and Trinity Bay in the teeth of the increasing gale. We hove-to near Split Point, Baccalieu Tickle to double reef our mainsail. While doing so we spotted a huge iceberg just north of Baccalieu Island. The "S.S. Home" passed by it on her way to St. John's coming from the north.

It was a tight haul to Catalina and as the wind was veering further to the north, the skipper decided to shake out a single reef of the Mainsail to speed up and try to reach Catalina before it got too bad. Meanwhile it was still blowing a heavy gale and snowing fast as well. In shaking out the double reef our reef tackle came unhooked and went flying over the taftrail and dropped in the sea some sixty or seventy feet from our schooner. We did not see it again.

With only a single reef in the mainsail now she was making better head-way with more sail to catch the wind. But it was not a pleasant sight to see the darkness coming on, and the water freezing on the riggings and sails.

We made Catalina safely and dropped the two anchors, cleared off the ice, tied up the canvas and turned in the bunk after a brief rest and supper.

At Catalina

Having reached Catalina safe and sound on Saturday night, November 21st., we were storm bound for two days, and did not get out until Saturday noon, November 23rd., when we set sail again and beat down as far as Northern Head, but the wind and sea were too heavy. There was a risk of losing our deck cargo; so the skipper decided to return back to Catalina as the other schooners were doing also.

Then on Sunday, a day on which the skipper was never anxious to sail, weatherwise we had no other choice; we got underway, hoisted the mainsail but let it drop again when a schooner came in and reported a very heavy sea outside. And the glass was still down.

We tried it again on Monday which looked like a good day for us. Bright and early we got up, and around nine o'clock we left Catalina with a boom-out time and managed to get a few miles beyond Cape Bonavista into the Bay when it began to snow with a change in the wind to a south east gale, heavy sleet snow, making visibility almost nil. We were making some progress and later picked up the sound of the foghorn on Puffin Island, Greenspond. From there we found our way under a reef foresail and jumbo into Port Nelson (Loo Cove) just before dark. There we were snowed in, with almost too much slob ice to get ashore to send a telegram home to let our people know where we were. And we needed to get some more fresh water in the keg.

Having anchored safely just outside Uncle Ned Blackwood's premises we haled Skipper John who called to us from his house. There were other vessels in port, and next morning we noticed the "Tukalu" (Skipper Jasper Chaulk), the "Undine" (Skipper Steve Goodyear) who came in behind us the previous evening, and one other schooner.

At Port Nelson and Away

Port Nelson is such a small place and with all the snow piled up around the hills, fences and the houses it looked as if we were shut in for the winter. However, after a day or so we managed to get ashore twice and visit our relatives there. Skipper John Blackwood and I went along with Duke Blackwood further up the Arm where he lived with his mother and two sisters.

His father and brothers were all lost at Northern Head, Catalina in the "Ella M. Rudolph" December 6th., 1926. All the crew were drowned, except Duke (that story forms another part of this book). We were nearly worn out at Port Nelson. A full week waiting for a time down and shovelling snow off the deck every morning. However, on Sunday again the morning dawned with the appearance of a good day. To the delight of all of us the skipper decided to get her underway again. Another boom-out time which lasted us almost down to the Gull Island, Cape Freels. There we were forced to bring over our foresail to starboard. The wind had changed a little further northern, and began to increase. The skipper said,

"Haul her in all you can and try to make the north side of Gull Island. Trim her right down, it's going to blow today before we gets down the Straight Shore. If we can get through the Run pass Edward's Reef and over towards Seldom we'll make it."

We were ahead, while the "Tukalu" and "Undine" came close behind us. Our vessel was a good sailor, but nothing was much good in this storm of heavy wind and sea. Every member of the crew took a short watch on deck, and had to be careful what he was doing or where he stood because the seas were coming right over us stem to stern and one had to be alert so as not to slip on the slob ice or get washed overboard. The glass had gone down four tenths below 29 and was still going down. The ocean was feather white.

We kept sailing, trimmed down to the last point, with what seemed like a rushing speed with every sea spraying from stem to stern washing the sidelights and going over the taffrail. It was hard staying on deck. Every time a big sea would strike someone gave an indication or sign that we should turn back. But that was a decision of the skipper and mate. Finally it got too tough and it was decided to turn back and try to make Lumsden (Cat Harbour) the nearest land and shelter (if it could be called such). At least we could anchor and be on the watch for a chance to get ashore. If we had to go to sea, nobody could tell what would happen. We were almost down to the South Penguin Island, and we might have gotten as far as Peckford Island Bight, but it might have been many nights like the other schooners that were out in the same storm. They were driven miles off course, and had to be rescued by steamers who went out looking for them when the news broke of several schooners not making port that day.

We Arrived at Lumsden

After deciding to heave back, and shortening sail, we reached Lumsden just before dark and dropped our two anchors in what we thought was the best place. We could hardly see where we were, due to the heavy wind, sea and snow. However, the skipper being in there many times, he used what vision he had and figured it was the best he could do under the circumstances.

The other two schooners followed us, and anchored just a little inside of us which seemed to have better holding ground. The "Elare", (Skipper Aquilla Hicks) had been there nearly all week waiting for a trip home to Carmanville.

Now there were four schooners in Lumsden all from Carmanville, and knew each other very well. As it was now dark and very stormy there wasn't much we could do except watch and prepare to get on shore next morning in case we had to leave the vessel.

After we got settled away and the watches arranged for the night, the cook, Pierce Blackwood managed to get some supper for us. The cup of tea, nice and warm, refreshed us and we felt like lying down, but there was no chance of doing so. It was too stormy and the vessel was in a constant motion. Our anchors were jumping and dragging over the bottom by the heavy weight of the vessel. We had shifted out of our first position and were now out near the Seal, or Middle Rocks where the heavy seas used to come so close to the stern of the "Erema" and send her ahead with such force and back again like a see-saw, back and forth. The wind and snow with such sea force would put her rail under water. It was difficult to move around on deck and keep things in place. We spent the long night as if we were in a dark cave with a roaring noise of sea and wind all around us.

Every crew member was dressed fully in all the warm clothes possible, as well as oil skins. It seemed to have gotten worse after midnight. Just before daylight I was below in the forecastle putting in a junk of wood to keep the fire going when I heard a sudden bang like a cannon in the fore peak. What a grinding sound! I started up the ladder to go on deck, when Uncle Charlie shouted out at me,

"Come on, the schooner is all adrift. The chains are broken, and we are in the seas. Hurry up!"

I rushed up but didn't know where I was going or what to do until I heard uncle Steve say

"Roland, jump out in the motor boat," (which they hurried over the lee rail).

"We are going to try and get ashore somewhere if we can."

I rushed aft to where the motor boat was bobbing up and down in the sea. I jumped right in the boat on the fore-shut, the others followed very quickly with the skipper last. I glanced around in the dull twilight and saw through the snow storm and wind the rolling furious seas splashing up on the beach and rocks around us everywhere. The other three schooners were tossing about like toys. The ghost of the grim reaper seemed everywhere, and ready for us.

It didn't take long to get away from the stranded vessel so as not to be caught in the wake and swamped. It certainly was a fight for life, and fortunately for us the six horesepower Acadia engine in our boat started with the first turn of the fly-wheel. That was a miracle, because nearly all night Uncle Steve was trying to get it to go. It had been frozen up for a day or two, but he worked on it with boiling water the night before, and finally got it free. (There was no anti-freeze in those days for local schooners). Now that the engine was going we made our way clear of the "Erema" and headed for the beach.

I saw our schooner when she struck the rocks on South Cat Harbour Island just minutes after we left her. I saw the seas go right over her and the keel forward came out of the water, while her two spares tipped right down on the rocks. The second sea, and the next passed over her completely, with pieces of canvas scattering all around and washing upon the rocky beach. "She became a total loss." Her cargo designated for Botwood and other northern ports was now strewn all along the beach of Southern Cat Harbour Island, Lumsden, which the fishermen would be able to pick up and salvage as soon as the storm abated and they were able to get out to that island. Of course some of it drifted out to sea on the westerly winds.

We grabbed little personal things as we were about to leave. I had a small clothes bag and the skipper snatched the weather glass off the cabin wall and a small compass in case we needed it. What a lot of things went to the bottom! A general cargo of food, clothing ... all kinds of merchandise.

Meanwhile, we beat our way amidst the heavy sea and strong wind towards the beach at Lumsden North the safest place to land. Finally we landed and some men were waiting on the shore to rescue us. We landed somewhere near a small cove, and they signalled to us to land at the old F.P.U. wharf.

They soon helped us up and took care of us in their homes, while others were planning how to get the other schooner crews ashore.

They were in a little smoother water away from the sea, but they all wanted to get ashore, because they were afraid any minute the vessels would go adrift and their fate would be the same as ours. The skipper and Uncle Steve decided to take a chance at it and off they went again to the "Elrae", the nearest one, and rescued the crew. They did the same for the others until everyone was safely landed. Our boat proved a life-boat for all of us, and we thanked God. The skipper and Uncle Steve were near exhaustion when the rescue was over, and permitted the Lumsden fishermen to pull in the motor boat and store it for the winter.

The other three crews waited for a time home but some fourteen days passed before they were able to get home.

The people of Lumsden were very kind. Uncle Charlie, Edward, and I were taken in and looked after by a Mr. Jones Wright; we dried our clothes, lay down by the stove in the warm and almost went to sleep when we were called up to come to the table for breakfast. I remember it was delicious, plenty of warm tea, bread and very tasty watered fish. What a meal after so long without a warm cup of tea, more than twenty-four hours! When the meal was finished, we lay back again by the stove which was giving off a good heat and soon fell asleep. A well deserved nap. The other crews were taken in by the people of Lumsden, and treated the same.

Ready for Home

I had just awakened from sleep when I heard a voice asking if Roland Abbott was there.

Someone answered and said yes.

It was Mr. Isaac W. Abbott from Musgrave Harbour. He was going down home and offered me a ride on his horse and sleigh. He had been up that way when he brought Mr. and Mrs. William Parsons to Lumsden to visit their daughter Mrs. John Abbott. It was the depth of winter, snow piled high all along the path, and the ponds frozen solid. All down the shore the going was good. It was quite a contrast from out on the ocean.

At Deadman's Bay we went in to Mr. William Goodyear's and had a cup of warm tea. Then on again down the shore chatting and looking out at the rough seas where we had been two days before.

We stopped for a few minutes at Anchor Brook, and told Mr. John Powell the story of my experience the last three or four days. We did not tarry long as we were anxious to get home before dark and the weather coming on with more snow and cold.

When we got to High Point on the shore, we met my father and John Peddle on our own horse, "Bess". They passed us on their way to Lumsden to bring me home, and would have gone on not seeing me; until uncle Isaac called them back and told them he was bringing me home. I was lying back at the time trying to keep as warm as I could. They came back since there were two of them, I stayed with Mr. Abbott. At that time the rescuer was responsible for the safe custody of wrecked crews which they were escorting to their homes, so for that reason as well, I stayed with Isaac Abbott.

Finally we arrived home safe and sound, glad to be with my family again. The round trip began on October 21st, and ended December 2nd, 1929. I was 16.

Returned to my Home

I was the first one of the crew to return home after thirty-six days on a trip that usually took about six or seven days to go and come. But this being an exceptionally stormy fall, one could almost expect anything in the way of trouble. It certainly happened this year!

Several people were at the house next morning before I was up. They were there to hear the story of our long trip and the shipwreck at Lumsden, which I had to tell over and over to other visitors who came in later. My father's brother, Uncle Jabez was very interested, as others were who had experiences on the sea and at the seal hunt.

Meanwhile, the other members of our crew came home later, some on the "S.S. Home" the coastal boat, while the skipper came up the shore several days after all the wreckage was cleared up, and the business part settled with the insurance and freight owners.

The "S.S. Home" on her way north next trip called in at Lumsden, and when ready took the three schooners "Undine", "Tuckalu", and "Elrae" in tow hoping to bring them to Carmanville. But it was too much for the schooners. The towling rigged to the three vessels almost tore them apart and nearly dismasted the one in the center. However, the "Undine" closest to the "Home" was to be towed to Carmanville, but it was a difficult tow as it was still stormy.

The "Tuckalu" got towed to Carmanville next time, and the "Elrae" made it on her own. Skipper Aquilla came up very close to the shore in a storm and was ready to beach her if it came to the worst, but made it safe to Carmanville.

After we got ashore that morning, the news broke that several schooners were driven off in the storm; some were resuced, and the crews taken off by steamers which were sent out to help the stranded vessels, while others got in up on the South Coast under their own power and sails. The "Neptune II" (Captain Job Barbour) drifted all the way across the Atlantic Ocean over to North Scotland, and got towed into Oban by the "S.S. Hesperus"!

Conclusion

Now that my story is ended, I will include the poem that I wrote shortly after I came home. I should say that after Christmas I accepted a school and went teaching on January 7th. The poem is as follows:

THE LOSS OF THE "EREMA H."

1. Come all ye brave young fishermen,
   And traders of the sea;
   While I'll relate some lines to you,
   About a young boy who fought the breeze.
   Twas in the "Erema H.", a fine old ship,
   And a very good sailor, too.
   Her skipper's name was Blackwood
   while I was one of the crew.

2. First, for the crew who were on board;
   To you I'll read each name.
   There was skipper Theophilus Blackwood
   From Carmanville he came.
   Four others from that place belong,
   Stephen, Charlie and Pierce.
   Ned Ellsworth in his middle age,
   Was counted not the worse.

3. Now just for one more little chap
   From Musgrave Harbour came,
   Who acted very well that trip,
   Roland Abbott was his name.

   He fought the gales like all the rest
     without a sign or moan;
   But everyone was happy
     When he arrived safe home.

4. On the twenty-first day of November,
     The "Erema" left the town.
   Full load of heavy cargo,
     For Botwood, we were bound.
   With a gentle breeze of about West,
     Our schooner sailed along;
   Then it began to blow a gale,
     And night was coming on.

5. Near twelve o'clock that very day
     We had to reef our sails.
   Down Trinity Bay the wind did gust,
     And all showed signs of gales.
   When Split Point then we were abreast
     The mainsail it was reefed,
   And we tried to do our very best
     To reach home without any grief.

6. We reached Catalina just after dark,
     The wind was at its height;
   But all, the skipper and the crew
     were glad to harbour that night.
   On Monday morning when we came out
     It was a boom out time,
   Until we reached across the Bay,
     And no fear was on our mind.

7 Late in the evening that very day,
     Port Nelson it was reached;
   While under our foresail and jumbo,
     We sailed close to the beach.
   But we were glad and full of glee,
     And to make this song a rhyme;
   We were now safe in harbour
     With the "Tukalu" and "Undine".

8. It rained, it snowed and then it blew.
　　In Port Nelson, a week we passed,
　On Sunday morning we left again;
　　Below twenty-nine was our glass. (Barometer)
　We sailed along the Cape Freels shore;
　　It looks a beautiful time,
　The booms were swung across her,
　　But soon increased the wind.

9. While very early on that day,
　　Gull Island was quickly passed.
　So all was going well my boys,
　　And she was sailing fast.
　The wind was still increasing now,
　　'Twas dangerous to go on.
　We then decided to return, and beat
　　Back to Lumsden; which didn't take too long.

10 Now sad to say of what befell,
　　As did our anchors strain;
　When trying to put Catch Anchors out,
　　'Twas then she burst'd her chain.
　"Come on now boys" the call was then;
　　Without calling more than twice.
　"Come on," "Come on," jump in the boat
　　And we'll try to save our life."

11 In less than half an hour,
　　She was pounding on the rocks,
　The only thing we had time to take,
　　Was a suitcase, bag or box.
　Well, now before I finish,
　　The truth to you I'll tell;
　The loyal, kind friends of Lumsden,
　　They treated us very well.

12. They were so kind to us my lads;
      That goes for one and all.
   We thank them very sincerely
      For their kindness there that Fall.
   I'll now conclude and finish
      But our thanks to God for all.
   I ended my trip in the "Erema"
      After a month and half last Fall.

                    By: R.W. Abbott, Crew member.
                    Ship wrecked: December 2nd., 1929

The Erema H., at wharfside, St. John's. She was lost December 2, 1929, in a storm at South Cat Harbour Island, Lumsden, Newfoundland.

The loss of the Schooner 'Mollie'

December, 1944

Chapter 1.
Author's Note

The story of the "Ella M. Rudolph", and the "Erema H." even, were different from the story of the "Mollie". All three are close to our family, especially my late mother, in whose memory I was most inspired to write about all three, because she had been so concerned with the sad tragedies in her family relationship. And for the "Erema H." because I was the young member of the crew during that terrible night and following day when we were taken off the wreck.

However, the story of the "Mollie" seemed to attract my attention and deeper concern in following the sad and mysterious episode, a tragedy that clouded the minds of all who were involved with the ill-fated schooner and crew. Similar fate had occurred time and time again during our long era of ships and men at sea.

I knew Skipper Jasper Chaulk, Ross' father, back in 1929, when we were storm bound in Port Nelson (Loo Cove), and later sailed with him from Carmanville to Twillingate. During the trip, while going through the ships run before reaching Change Island End, I swung a plank over the stern of the "Mollie" and repainted her name there at the request of Skipper Jap, as we sailed smoothly along the run.

Later in October, 1944, I was at Horwood when the "Mollie" came in and tied up at the Horwood Lumber Co. Ltd. wharf in a storm. Skipper Ross was waiting to take on lumber for St. John's. While there I went aboard for a chat, and Uncle Jack Goodyear, Reggie and Charlie came up to our house and had tea with my wife and family. That was the last time we ever talked with them. Uncle Jack said then, he wished they were giving up for the fall, but wanted to make another trip to settle up, and get in a few more things for the winter. We did not suspect anything would so happen as it did, and that it was our last good-bye.

And so I went about to piece together for the records what I knew or could gather about the "Mollie's" last voyage. Much of the tale is the first hand information which I gathered from my Aunt Mary Goodyear who lost her husband and two sons in the tragedy. She told it from the beginning to the end as only she could do.

Then, while talking to Mrs. Nellie Chalk, Ross' mother, she told her sad story, and one could not but enter in, and feel the whole episode re-occurring again. I wish that I could have better expressed in my story the whole scene of her anxiety as she portrayed it to me in the interview while she and her son Ford went back over the pass of that terrible, sad event when the "Mollie" was lost. She supplied me with all the information she could think of and the pictures of the schooner and her son Skipper Ross.

The map of the scene at Grate's Cove, I copied from one done by a Mr. David Vey for The Thistle Family of that town and sent to Oswald Goodyear of the Goodyear crew members.

I also obtained a verbal account of the wreckage, and recovery of the bodies of the "Mollie" from Mr. Andrew Lewis when I visited the scene sometime after the accident as mentioned in my write-up.

Meanwhile I wish to acknowledge with thanks all who supplied me with information. Mrs. Goodyear, Mrs. Chaulk, Albert Blackwood for a copy of the Family Fireside Newspaper 1945 with the Gerald S. Doyle News Bulletin relating the eventful tragedy. Mrs. Nina Tulk for a picture of her brother James Ellsworth, mate. Mrs. J. Guy for the poem by the late Willis Tulk, and Mr. Kenneth Hicks. Also the many casual chats with other folks relating to the incident.

Roland W. Abbott,
Author

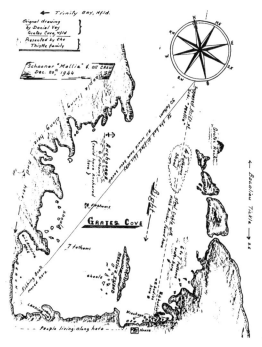

Chapter 2
The Chaulks

Chaulk is a surname of England, from Chalke (Wiltshire) or Chalk (Kent). In Newfoundland a John Chaulk (about 1753-1838) was the first settler of Bird Island Cove (now Elliston). Some of the Chaulks settled at Bonavista, a Richard Chaulk at Fogo 1803, and a Richard Chaulk at Deadman's Bay about 1858.

It is probably the Richard of Deadman's Bay who is the early ancestor of the Chaulks whose line we may be connected with in this story; the line of our more recent ancestors, and those relatives of my mother and the Chaulks here. They were: Elias Chaulk, who is my great grandfather on my mother's side. He married Louisa Gudcher (Goodyear) on May 30, 1855 at Cat Harbour (now Lumsden) not far from Deadman's Bay. Louisa was sister to Jerimah (Jerry) Goodyear of Cape Freels, and later of Deadman's Bay.

Their family consisted of: Stephen, William II, Robert II, Fanny (my grandmother), (George Blackwood), Janet (Edwin Tulk) and Lucy (Simon Day).

Now to follow the family of Elias mentioned above, and then his son Stephen II (my grandmother's brother) known at Carmanville as "Uncle Steve Chaulk", married Hellen (Nellie) Gray of Cat Harbour (Lumsden) at Cat Harbour in the school chapel on October 25, 1876. They raised their family at Deadman's Bay, and later at Rocky Bay (now Carmanville) which consisted of: Elias II, Henry, Richard II, Alpheus, John II, Jasper, Alice and Laura.

Jasper, the son of Stephen II, married Helen (Nellie) Goodyear of George from Carmanville south. Their family were five boys and five girls. The boys were: Maxwell, Donald, Ross, Ray and Ford. The girls were Ruby, Minty, Hazel, Ruth and May.

Chapter 3
Their Trade

The Chaulks of Elias; Stephen, Jasper and Ross were fishermen, or seamen, and naturally were spending much of their working time in boats on the sea—from the smaller fishing boat to the Bully (a three sail boat), and later the schooner. The Chaulks stepped higher, bigger, and farther out to sea; even to Labrador, and the several harbours up there to fish with hook, lines, and cod traps; which for a while seemed to be fairly prosperous, and netted a good income for that day.

But this traditional trade, fishing, began to decline both in productivity and value, all of which made it more difficult, and was even labour in vain. Toiling all day and late at night getting little or nothing in return. Therefore, it became almost useless to leave Carmanville or any harbour on the coast to go to Labrador with not much to look forward to for the winter.

Elias and Stephen were both just about finished with it having grown older, the life did not appeal to them in their declining years. Jasper too, felt the change in life's style and decided to try another way of life. He turned to the coasting trade or freight carrying from port to port, lumber, salt, limestone, and general merchandise from St. John's to coves and harbours; even as far north as St. Anthony. For this kind of business he purchased a schooner of about 45 tons called the "Tukalou". He had a most trying experience in this vessel when caught in a terrible storm at Cat Harbour (Lumsden) in December, 1929, and had to be towed home to Carmanville by the "S.S. Home", Captain Thomas Hounsell in charge. However, she was later lost and became a total wreck off Noggins Cove Head, near Carmanville.

Meanwhile, earning a livelihood had to continue and coastal trading was now his means of doing so, and he decided to buy another schooner bigger this time, if he could get one to suit him and his pocket book. There was a very fine, good looking schooner tied up at a south side wharf in St. John's which Skipper Jasper heard of, and spied out for himself. She was for sale, and Skipper Jasper was successful in getting her; an 85 ton vessel called the "Mollie".

Chapter 4.
The "Mollie"

The "Mollie" was built in Lunenberg, Nova Scotia, and did trading business from Quebec to Hanley Harbour, Labrador coast, skippered by Captain George Whiteley, who bought her around the year 1905. She was then painted white, with green bottom, and carried two topmasts dressed with mainsail, foresail, jumbo, jib, flying jib, gaft topsail, and topmast staysail; very slick looking indeed when all sails set, "a fine sailor" it was said.

It was in the early 30's, and trading began to slow down too, with a depression appearing on the economical horizon, but still one had to carry on; which he did even with a world war raging in the late decade and early 40's and the sea lanes becoming dangerous with submarines and mines even in and near the coastal waterways. Skipper Jap (as he became locally known among his contemporaries) became ill and could not carry on any longer as master of his vessel. Before the time came around again to sail for the ensuing season, he passed away, May 14th, 1941, leaving the "Mollie" to his sons to continue the coasting trade if they could or wanted to.

Meanwhile, somehow or another, before he died he seemed to want his son Ross to become master of the "Mollie". Ross had adapted a different trade or avocation. He was a telegraph operator at Musgrave Harbour, but was hardly content or happy with that and on the land. His interest was on the sea, in boats, sea life and soon he found himself taking a marine test or examination no. 307 which he passed on March 5th, 1943, signed by the chief examiner R.C. Sheppard at the port of St. John's. He also passed his vision test on March 2nd, 1943. He then joined the coastal boat, M.V. "Henry W. Stone", March 13, 1943 as a sailor, but was discharged April 6, 1943 and later joined the "S.S. Glencoe" as an able seaman. However, to carry out his father's wish to master the "Mollie", he left the "Glencoe", and was discharged March 18, 1944 with a V.G. (very good) character report for ability and general conduct.

Chapter 5
Skipper Ross in Charge

Skipper Ross Chaulk fitted out the "Mollie" in the spring of 1944, an early start to continue the coasting trade, which his late father had done for several years. Ross sailed with him too, and now had sufficient sea time to master the "Mollie" with the help of his crew who signed on for the ensuing season.

Meanwhile, World War II was at its height, especially at sea, and along the north and east coast of Newfoundland where Skipper Ross' trade route lay, it was certainly very dangerous.

The Anglo Newfoundland Development Company at Grand Falls was in the paper making business, and the Buchans Mine produced mineral concentrates; these were shipped through the seaport of Botwood, and the ships of necessity for safety or protection had to be escorted and join in convoy with other ships for overseas markets.

Meanwhile, Skipper Ross in the "Mollie" went about their coastal trading to St. John's picking up freight for the nothern outports, and returning to St. John's with lumber from Horwood Lumbering Co., Horwood, Newfoundland,

It was during one of those trips or voyages that Skipper Ross Chaulk in the "Mollie" was outside St. John's one very stormy night in the late fall. It was war-time, and he was not given permission to enter the harbour. The "Mollie" arrived off St. John's toward evening, and hopefully would get in before dark. The forecast was not too good, and predicted a heavy storm outside, or off St. John's shore which would not be a very pleasant place to spend a dark stormy night, battering thick snow or heavy seas. Skipper Ross was anxious as well as his crew to get in the harbour and tie up to some wharf so that they could rest from long hours of watching on the recent trip south.

Off St. John's

However, since this was war-time, and all necessary precautions were taken by the authorities to keep St. John's Harbour protected from enemy action a heavy chain was strung across The Narrows, the natural entrance to the harbour. Therefore, an escort was necesssary to get all vessels into the important harbour, especially toward late evening when security was tight.

It is understood Skipper Ross gave the necessary signals to the shore base on Signal Hill requesting permission or an escort to enter The Narrows and into St. John's Harbour which he thought would be granted since his vessel was a local coaster. However, despite all his efforts for permission to enter, he was flatly denied and had to heave off and remain outside St. John's all night.

A Bad Night at Sea

It was a terrible night at sea, with darkness and trying to cope with the heavy seas, high winds and sleety rain. It battered the "Mollie" and crew too, terribly. They were often angry at the way they were treated by the authorities, as if they were enemies, while other times they were praying for their safety and daylight to enter the harbour and hoping that the "Mollie" would survive the terrible beating she was receiving from the wild storm and heavy seas. It shook her from stem to stern making her hull leak until the water rose up above the cabin floor.

Captain Ross and his crew spent the dark night on deck keeping watch for any ship that might be also in the area; and more important perhaps to keep the vessel off the land. In the daylight next morning before they were allowed in the harbour in a battered condition with much of the deck load of lumber gone overboard and the canvas (sails) badly damaged. Captain Chaulk reported the serious matter to the authorities, but it didn't cure the damage or compensate him for the terrible night at sea. It was certainly an unfair act.

Last Trip North

However, Captain Ross Chaulk of the "Mollie" had to keep going. It meant bread and butter on the table for him and his crew. And so another trip was made from St. John's to the northern ports, then with a load of lumber back to the capital.

He had planned to be home and tied up in mid-December or at least before Christmas. But due to bad weather, and a very stormy fall they were delayed and he found himself as late as December 19th, 1944 before he could clear the St. John's Narrows for his home at Carmanville which would take him, in the "Mollie", a couple of days to reach with a good time along. The fall of 1944 was not good weatherwise, and misfortune seemed to dodge the "Mollie".

Chapter 6
In St. John's

The "Mollie" often lay waiting or discharging freight or general merchandise at Ayre & Sons, St. John's wharf. Orders to ship on the "Mollie" this or that were coming in continually from outport merchants of the north, and coming down the wharf every day on horse and cart, truck or being pushed down on hand cart until every part of the hull, was filled, and the cabin blocked as well. even, it is said, the forecastle, where the crew had to eat and sleep. The bunks were filled and the crew had to eat on the corners of the table. The "Mollie" was heavily laden. Skipper Ross did not like to refuse anyone from getting a much needed commodity on his vessel as long as there was an inch of space. Much of the general cargo was for Horwoods, at Horwood, Notre Dame Bay, while the deck load of hay was for the Gander Bay merchants in the lumbering business. The skipper and his crew were very anxious to get out, hoping for a good time home, with this the last trip for the season. It would mean a good Christmas with a little extra on the menu from a financial standpoint.

Ready to Leave

The "Mollie" with her heavy burden of all assortments of general merchandise, six brave seamen; Captain Ross Wilson Chaulk, age 26, unmarried; Mate James Ellsworth Jr., age 25, unmarried; John F. Goodyear, age 61, married, and his two sons Reginald, age 32, Charles, age 26, both unmarried, and Otto Hicks of Musgrave Harbour, a widower with one child. All were ready and anxious to get out of the harbour and to be homeward bound.

The final item arrived on board, repaired canvas now in good condition, the "Mollie" could be dressed to suit the calm or storm and face the north seas." "We are ready now, Skipper," said the mate. "Yes, tomorrow morning as soon as possible we'll try and get her out of this." And tomorrow morning the 18th of December, 1944 the "Mollie" under little motor power and sail glided out The Narrows, turned northward and making good time reached the Sugar Loaf, and almost to Torbay, when it began to snow. Soon the wind chopped (veered or changed from the northwest) which of course was dead against the vessel. Using his good judgement he turned around and took the "Mollie" back to St. John's to await a better time.

December 19, 1944

The next day December 19th, it looked much better, the wind and snow had stopped, so weatherwise a fair time home. Just after daylight which that time of year would be well up toward eight-thirty, the skipper called up the crew, and ordered the lines to be untied from the wharf grumps, the small motor engine in the cabin started and the canvas set once more (and for the last time) moving the "Mollie" down the harbour towards The Narrows. Now the course was set down St. John's shore toward Baccalieu Tickle across Conception Bay and on to Catalina before dark or shortly afterward. That leg of the journey would be a great advantage and one or two more at least would land them safely home. That's how it usually had to be done in late fall from port to port sailing during the daylight only and watching the wind and weather. December 19th, was rather a fine steady day at the beginning. The water was not too rough after the previous day's up wind, and now a very light southerly wind made the "Mollie" with her precious cargo move down St. John's shore to Torbay then Cape St. Francis and across the waters of Conception Bay, about three o'clock to reach Baccalieu Tickle, well over half way to the next harbour, Catalina, where they could anchor for the night.

Baccalieu Tickle 4:00 P.M.

It seems that the "Mollie" that day was the lone vessel in that area, and attracted the attention of the folks at Bay de Verde, who, seemingly could not help but comment on the single sailing vessel heading north. Many watched her out of sight and into the darkness of the fall evening. They saw her until around four o'clock as she passed on through the Tickle, northward bound followed by a very light wind.

Chapter 7
At Carmanville December 19, 1944

With a late fall evening of early darkness settling over the harbour and homesteads there is a sense of loneliness among all the folks, and thoughts turn to those who are not yet at home. The chores of the day being finished, the firewood brought in and stowed in the wood box, the water barrel filled, the animals in the barns tied up and fed for the night, the supper by lamp light is over and the dishes put back. The usual house calls and neighbourly visits then occur to exchange news of the day and it was now time to listen on radio to the war news, followed by the Gerald S. Doyle news bulletin 'bringing you the news from all over Newfoundland', including hospital reports and the forecast. But of great importance and interest to many folks of Carmanville at this time was the schooner or shipping reports as to their whereabouts if they left a particular harbour or arrived at a certain time. Two or three vessels from Carmanville were still at sea somewhere and expected home any day. The "Neva Belle," Captain Frank Collins, The "Mazeltov," Captain Stephen Goodyear, and the "Mollie," Captain Ross Chaulk.

Although the day was fairly quiet and calm for an early winter December day, there were signs of snow and easterly wind on the horizon toward evening. As night wore on snow was on the way and a scattered flake fell, increasing until towards mid-night it was snowing heavily and began to drift with an increased wind. A blinding snow storm was raging. It lasted well into the next day December 20, 1944.

Goodyear's House

Meanwhile, as night advanced and most people were at home so was the Goodyear family, Oswald and his mother, while John the husband and sons Reggie and Charlie were on the "Mollie" homeward bound. Oswald knew his mother was uneasy.

She said, "My Oswald, your father and them got a bad night tonight if they're out."

"Yes," said Oswald "but I guess they got to Catalina if they didn't run up in the bay and got in a small harbour and couldn't send a message or were too late to send it when they got in. It's kind of a bad night all right."

"I suppose Uncle Steve Goodyear and Captain Frank (Collins) are out too somewhere."

The conversation was not long. There was not much to talk about or do, only retire and listen to the heavy wind blowing, to fall off to sleep, and later waken from the snow and wind, thinking and thinking, and wait the verdict of daylight and morning; which was indeed very stormy up until after noon, and into evening before one could get out around and clear away the snow. Everyone as they met mentioned the storm: Oswald to console his mother, said "I guess Skipper Ross will send his mother a message today letting her know his whereabouts." The Goodyears sat silently and worried.

Chaulk's House

At Chaulk's house too the night was a long anxious one. Uncle Harry Chaulk, and Aunt Blanche Chaulk (of John) were at Ross' house talking to his mother and members of the family. Most of their conversation concerned Ross and the "Mollie" and news of their possible whereabouts. Uncle Harry and Aunt Blanche went home (just a few feet away from each other in the family garden) because it looked like heavy weather was coming on.

Mrs. (Jasper) Nellie Chaulk, Ross' mother, continued her knitting after her brother-in-law, and sister-in-law left. But just for a little while before she moved around the house, to the door, to the window, and added some wood to the kitchen stove to prepare a cup of warm tea before retiring. Yet, deep in thought of the "Mollie" and Ross wondering where they were, "did he leave St. John's I wonder? I guess he did because it was a nice morning and a light southerly breeze. He might have got to Catalina too late to let me know. He said on his Christmas card he sent me a few days ago that he would be home in a day or two, and home for Christmas."

However, the night wore on and towards midnight Mrs. Chaulk went to bed to wait for morning, but she could not rest. Just after 12 o'clock she said,

"I got out of bed to look out the window, but I couldn't see anything it was mad rough. I said to Ruth, my daughter, 'My what a bad night. I'm so uneasy, I wonder where is Ross. If he's out tonight, he's certainly into it, if 'tis as bad up St. John's way as it is down here. My it's terrible, snowing and blowing a gale. He'll never do anything with it tonight. Oh my! Oh my! I wonder why did he stay so long in St. John's. He shouldn't have gone up the last trip' " — now she began to repeat some of her former remarks.

"What a terrible night to be out, I daresay he's out though, because t'was such a fine morning for this time of the year, and no doubt he was anxious to get out of St. John's and get home if he could. I hope he got over to Catalina. Perhaps, I'll get a message tomorrow, saying he got in all right."

With the conversation ended, there was a strange silence, except for the roar of the storm outside, and with the hope it would be better in the morning with news of the "Mollie" safe in harbour, Mrs. Chaulk lay down again, hoping to sleep, but dreams of dread and premonitions would not allow her to do so.

Ellsworth's House

At the Ellsworth house it was similar, Mr. and Mrs. Edward Ellsworth were also concerned about their son, James who was mate on the "Mollie." They lived on the outer most part of the harbour, called Noggins Cove Head, and felt the full brunt of the storm, of snow and a hurricane of wind shaking the very foundation of the old homestead, while they sat and listened around the kitchen stove. They did not converse too much, silent with their thoughts and mind far to the south, St. John's, Conception Bay, Baccalieu Tickle, Trinity Bay and Catalina Harbour.

Those places held their attention, and visualizing in the darkness the "Mollie", her crew, and especially "Jim", Uncle Ned Ellsworth could easily see in fancy the whole ocean scene around that area, because he had spent many nights similar to this one. This was the worst he could remember, although he had a lot of sea time to his credit. The night of terror in December 1929 when the schooner "Erema H." became a total loss at Lumsden during a blizzard of snow and gale force wind, he escaped with the crew in a small motor boat, but he was younger then. Now this night was one of agony to him, his son Jim, only 26 years old, somewhere out in the darkness on a vessel at sea so there's no peace of mind. He comforted his dear wife with words of encouragement. They lay down to rest but as with many other folks of Carmanville, could not sleep. The storm was too furious.

Musgrave Harbour

At the home of Otto Hicks and in Musgrave Harbour the same anxious feelings were not so pronounced. He was a widower, and his only child being so young did not have any idea of what was going on or where her dad was at the time. However his relatives were not fully aware if he was on the "Mollie" or not, or if he was coming on the

"S.S. Glencoe" with his father, Edward, who was in St. John's at the time and ready to come home. But he told his father he was going down on the "Mollie" with Skipper Ross, and next year he was hoping to join her as a crew member. Meanwhile, the folks of Musgrave Harbour had some concern for those in ships on the sea, especially those from the neighbouring community of Carmanville since a lot of the people were related and others used to sail on the Carmanville schooners in the coasting trade. The people of Musgrave Harbour had experienced many storms and seen a like number of shipwrecks over the years even with loss of life, so the storm was felt by the people on the straight shore as it blew in from the great seaway of the North Atlantic. As they said, "a wild night at sea."

Chapter 8
Grate's Cove December 19, 1944

The people of Bay de Verde and Grate's Cove had seen many a vessel pass north and south along the high headlands of their rugged coast, and through Baccalieu Tickle in all kinds of weather winter and summer. They saw them during daylight, and their lights at night if it wasn't too foggy or stormy. The usual remarks passed were, "That's a big one," or "That little fellow will hardly make it," "Boy, them fellows are going to have a bad night tonight, if they don't get in somewhere."

Conversations or remarks of this kind were spoken because they themselves lived near the sea, and wrestled their livelihood from often stormy waters. They had an interest and concern for those trading back and forth.

This time a sailing schooner was making her way north and the people who looked seaward and out towards Baccalieu Island from Bay de Verde saw her. They learned it was the "Mollie" going through the Tickle, and as Mr. Paul Emberly postmaster at Bay de Verde told the author, he saw her about four o'clock or just about dark slowly sailing northward through the Tickle. Since Bay de Verde and Grate's Cove are not too far apart the people of Grate's Cove heard that a schooner was in the Tickle late evening going north, but no one knew her exact whereabouts after that. They, no doubt thought the usual procedure was followed: go on to Catalina and harbour for the night, or if it was a favourable time, proceed to the home port. The evening didn't look too bad, just one of those fall evenings, yet there was a strange calmness.

Concert at Grate's Cove

Mr. Andrew Lewis, of Grate's Cove, who at that time was just 29 years old, told me when I visited him later,

"On the night of December 19th, 1944, the night the "Mollie" passed through Baccalieu Tickle bound north, the children were having their Christmas Concert in the school room, an annual event just before school closed for the Christmas holidays. The program was hardly finished, that might have been around nine thirty or close to ten o'clock; when it began to snow, lightly at first, a few blossoms, but soon increased with drifts swirling around the corner of the school as the wind increased." But they managed, he said, to get all the children home just in time before it got really bad and expressing it as "mad rough in a short time." Before midnight it was getting worse. His neighbours came in to say how bad it was and thought they should go over on the north side, and pull in their boats for safety; which they did, and, as he said, just made it, for by that time or around midnight you hardly could see a hand before your eyes. It was a blizzard, a real hurricane of north east wind with snow piling up two and three feet, whirling around the houses, stores, and over fences. It was a night to be at home and snugly sheltered. One would feel a little nervous fearing what might happen outside before daylight with such a storm raging. And thus the inhabitants of Grate's Cove were sheltered in their homes from the hurricane raging outside unaware of any tragedy occurring a short distance from their homes. They were unaware that the schooner which passed through the Tickle earlier in the evening with six on board was off their harbour, out in the bay, tossed about by wind, snow and heavy sea.

One can only imagine, using any experience or saga of the sea in similar circumstances, blinded by an unruly, spiteful snow storm and hurricane wind, not knowing their whereabouts, how dreadful it can be.

Chapter 9
The "Mollie" December 19, 1944

As we have said the "Mollie" made slow progress the first part of the day after leaving St. John's, and towards evening reached Baccalieu Tickle. It soon got dark on that late fall evening. Does it predict a brewing storm? It's a fair run from St. John's to harbour at Catalina in a sailing vessel with a little motor power on a short December day. With a light southerly breeze one could not hope to make that harbour before dark.

Now, what happened that evening and night after the "Mollie" went out of sight and possibly through the Tickle and out into Trinity Bay. No one survived to tell the tale. One can only imagine that night just before midnight the wind veered out easterly, and later unto north east with hurricane force and heavy sleety snow blinding and closing in all visibility.

The consensus of experienced skippers who sailed those waters many times is that possibly after the "Mollie" passed through the Tickle she was out in Trinity Bay, a few miles across before the storm broke; mildly at first as it usually does when changing from one direction to another. The "Mollie" hit the storm before it struck Grate's Cove.

Perhaps, Captain Ross discussed the situation with his mate and crew, as is usual in times like this. They might have decided, in view of the increasing wind and snow, to run up into Trinity Bay to some harbour on the north side, or return through the Tickle and into Conception Bay and heave to; await daylight and see if the storm would abate.

Onboard Conversation

What is done in a situation like this? Did they shorten sail? Reef? Try to head out north east to clear Bonavista Cape? Heave back and try to reach the calmer waters of Trinity Bay? Retrace their course, through Baccalieu Tickle round Split Point, Bay de Verde Head and take shelter under the scrapes or run up in Conception Bay? These are questions that will never be answered. They did not reach Trinity or Conception Bays, nor did they get through the Tickle. A battered vessel possibly falling off leaward soon will come to a halt and strike the leaward shore or reefs.

Now, the time has come to make a decision, and as we will never know the true story we might suppose the mate said to the skipper, "what do you plan to do"?

"Well," mate it's such a blizzard, dark as pitch, snowing and blowing a gale you can hardly stand on deck. It looks like we won't reach Catalina tonight with a hurricane of wind and a storm like this. Perhaps it will be alright to heave back, and go up in Conception Bay if we can make the Tickle. I don't think with this wind we can do anything with Trinity Bay. We may not be far enough across to clear the headlands with this wind direction, and if she's making much leeway we'll only barely get through the Tickle without stricking on Split Point or Bay de Verde land.

"So get all hands on deck, tell them to rig out as soon as possible and everyone watch and listen for the Baccalieu light or land, or anything if they hear it. But be sure to hold onto the riggings or something strong.

"Lash the man to the wheel, we'll take short turns, because he'll soon get sogged wet, and freeze up a night like this.

"Everyone on watch. This is a lot worse than the night off St. John's the Fall.

"I wish now we could have left St. John's a little earlier we might have made Catalina, even if it was after dark."

"Where do you think we're now skipper?" the mate or a crew member might have asked.

"I don't know for sure boy. I was hoping we might keep off land or get back in the lun (leeward) of Baccalieu Island until daylight. The storm might drop then. It's hard to know what to do right now or where we are. What time is it, I wonder?"

"Skipper boy 'tis a terrible night, and awful sea too, the water is awful tumbly and so quick. The wind must have been up from the nord all day."

"Yes, 'tis mad rough too, and freezing like guns. We'll have to try and get the ice off her in the morning or as soon as we can see what we're doing or where we are. I daresay it will lighten around four o'clock, 'tis usually better or worse around that time."

"Can't get much worse skipper. Boy, oh boy, what a night!"

"Is there any fire in? Keep a bit going to keep our mitts and clothes dry as much as possible. Is the water any smoother? If we're inside Baccalieu Island or in the Tickle it should be, but it don't seem like that. Tis still pretty rough. I hope she can stand up to it."

And so the night wore on. But we do not know for how long. If the storm broke on Grate's Cove around midnight the "Mollie" might have had it an hour or two earlier out to sea. They must then have been working their way back or making leeway towards the land and Grate's Cove, due to lack of power or loss of canvas. No one will ever know, or what time the vessel first touched land. Or, if they discovered at the time they were near land and dropped the anchors outside of the cove in which they were found, hoping to hold up until daylight.

Picture the "Mollie" tossing perhaps almost helpless and unmanageable due to little or no motor or sail power. The man at the wheel says, "She won't answer to the helm." The sail, if still up is so stiff with ice and snow the wind just slips off and the rigging and ropes are cakes of ice. The roll and toss of the vessel makes it impossible to do anything or move from one place on deck to another.

It could be the mate and a companion were up near the windlass or forecastle trying to see. The skipper and Mr. Goodyear with his two sons might be huddled near the cabin and wheel peering through the darkness and heavy snow hoping for the best, not saying too much, but thinking homeward no doubt.

When the "Mollie" struck, and the seas engulfed her, what happened to the crew, how they left the vessel, what their last words or the skipper's orders were, we will never know.

Chapter 10
Carmanville December 20, 1944

The night of December 19th, 1944 finally ended. The worry and anxiety wore on for the early part of the new day and the residents of Carmanville once more awoke to enter a dull, dim, gloomy day, still snowing but abating a little. Yet it seemed to speak of sadness. Everyone went about meeting each other with a sad greeting, as if something told of a disaster.

'A bad night boy. Wonder where the boys were last night!'

Neva Belle

The storm was abating somewhat, and about midday the joy of the folks in the east end of the community and especially for those of the crew of the "Neva Belle," (Captain Frank Collins) that schooner hove in sight. Through the heavy snow, they could see her coming in the harbour like a ghost ship out of nowhere, snow and ice covered. She was making her way to anchorage and to tie up for the winter. Anchors were dropped, the ice-bound sails lowered and lashed down. The crew were soon released to be with their families. Thank God for a safe return home. But it didn't look good last night after losing the light near Muddy Shag off Musgrave Harbour and hove to in the blizzard!

The "Neva Belle" got in, now where is the "Mazeltov" (Captain Steve Goodyear), and the "Mollie" (Captain Ross Chaulk)? Everyone was asking where they were and all were hoping Captain Collins might have seen them.

Everyone was anxious to hear what Captain Frank Collins had to say about his experience, and question him of his whereabouts or if he heard anything about the other schooners.

Captain Collins left Harbour Grace on the morning of the 19th, while the others left St. John's. He did not see them anywhere on his way down. Apparently he was ahead of them. That's why he was so far advanced and nearly home before the storm caught up with him, nevertheless keeping the "Neva Belle" out all night.

Carmanville December 20, 1944

The day seemed very short, and soon night fell again. It was toward evening before the storm finally abated and not much could be done to check around to see how things turned out, and no news came from the two schooners still not yet home. Meanwhile, everyone settled down for another night, and the usual routine of the community ensued. At least it was little more settled this night weatherwise. 'It will be better tomorrow and hopefully some news will be received from the schooners still out somewhere.'

Chapter 11
Grate's Cove December 20, 1944

The storm was also abating on December 20th, at Grate's Cove following that awful night, and the folks were venturing outdoors to clear away the snow and drift of last night. The children did not get to school early next morning until the paths and roads were opened up. Most folks were busy checking on the home chores and getting around to hear the local news.

Meanwhile Mr. Andrew Lewis, 29, who lived very close to the edge of the high hill overlooking the harbour, was the first man to venture out from his home to take a look out the Cove towards the ocean. To his great surprise, he saw the wreckage of some vessel all over the Cove sweeping around in the sea, and in the gulch to his right piled up four to five feet high. Wreckage of every description floating around the cove.

"What a sight!"

Wreckage everywhere, but no crew members of that vessel to be seen anywhere.

Mr. Lewis told the author that he went out to look around as was his usual custom after a storm. And the first thing to his view was the wreckage, and as reported in the January 1945 issue of "The Family Fireside" newspaper,

"A considerable quantity of wreckage had drifted ashore at Grate's Cove including part of a spar, some bales of hay, and other general cargo and a piece of board on which was the word "Mollie".

Mr. Lewis immediately spread the news around the cove and by this time others had spotted the wreckage too. At once they organized search parties to look around the shore in the hope of locating the crew, who it was thought might have made their way into one of the coves in the neighbourhood. But they searched and there was no sign of life or of bodies.

They then decided to lower some men down the cliff by ropes to search the gulch where much of the wreckage had piled up. But again without success. All that could be found was wreckage of every description. A saw on which were the initials "J.J.C." a part bag of hard bread marked "G.C. Herring Neck," and a man's coat in which there was a Salvation Army pin, and wallet with a name that looked like "Elmsworth" on the identification card. (The pin was that of Reginald Goodyear, a Salvation Army soldier of the Carmanville Corps).

It was obvious that the ill-fated vessel was the schooner "Mollie" which had left St. John's two days previously for northern parts.

The first news of this tragedy was a message from the Relieving Officer at Grate's Cove sent to Sir John Puddester, Commissioner for Public Health and Welfare on the afternoon of December 20th, which read, "Wreckage Schooner Mollie of St. John's drove ashore Grate's Cove today. No sign of crew."

Chapter 12
Carmanville December 21st.

At Carmanville, December 20th passed without incident, except the arrival of the "Neva Belle" and the storm abating. There was no news of Captain Steve Goodyear in the "Mazeltov" or of the schooner "Mollie."

December 21st dawned with the storm over, and the folks about their usual chores; when daylight faded and night covered the community once more, the "Gerald S. Doyle" News Bulletin would bring news from all over Newfoundland. Again the local news bulletin was the special feature of the evening and everyone tuned in and listened attentively. No one moved about or spoke very much while the news was on; except when some name or place was mentioned which happened to be familiar to the listener.

Oswald Goodyear, whose father and two brothers were on the schooner "Mollie" left his mother at home with her evening chores. He went next door to his Uncle Stephen Blackwood to have a little chat about the day and to listen to the news bulletin and afterwards make a comment or two about the same around the Province, but it happened a special item was broadcast as the announcer read "A schooner and all her crew lost at Grate's Cove late December 19th or early morning of the 20th. The name on a board "Mollie" picked up."

This was the first news to reach Carmanville regarding the disaster. Oswald and his Uncle Stephen went silent. He got up and went home to be with his mother. When Aunt Mary heard it they both broke down. Soon the Rev. G.W. Case, United Church Pastor came in to confirm the sad news of the loss of the "Mollie" and her crew.

For Mrs. Goodyear, it meant her husband, John and two sons Reginald and Charles were lost. Would their bodies be found? If only they could be found and brought home! Oh, how sad, how sad! What do they do now?

Friends called to express their sympathy and offer all help possible. Rev. Case went on to bring the sad news to Mrs. Chaulk, Ross's mother, and on down the road to the Ellsworth family. The sad news spread quickly, and all the town of Carmanville was stricken.

Musgrave Harbour December 21

 Musgrave Harbour was also stricken with the same tragedy because Mr. Otto Hicks, son of Edward was one of the Mollie's crew. He too met a watery grave. His family were not sure at first if he was on the "Mollie" or coming on the steamer with his father. His wife had died a year or two ago, and their little daughter, Blanche, was too young to understand or know about her father's death. Otto's brothers and sisters were also living in different communities either married or away working. One sister Mrs. Lewinsor Abbott however was still living at Musgrave Harbour.

Chapter 13
Grate's Cove December 20 - 21

Grate's Cove on December 20th, not much could be done because of heavy seas, with the storm not yet completely over. However, they had enough evidence now to know what schooner it was, and that the crew no doubt were all drowned.

As soon as the wind and sea went down the organized search parties got out their boats, and went over in the cove toward southern point where most of the wreckage seemed to have gathered, to search for the bodies ... to see if they were among the debris or out in the water where some wreckage was still floating apparently attached to riggings or ropes.

They kept up their search despite bad weather and heavy seas. Thirteen boats were out every day until December 23rd. That morning it was a little smoother and they recovered four bodies in the exact spot where the wreckage of the schooner was first noticed. The body of Mr. Otto Hicks was not found until the morning of December 26th, 1944. It was some distance away from the other four. He and another man were found further out where the anchors and chains were found.

The crews worked persistently through the Christmas season until finally their efforts were rewarded with success and all the bodies found.

They were then conveyed from Grate's Cove to Old Perlican where they were placed in caskets, and taken to the Orange Hall where they remained until Sunday when they were taken to their homes at Carmanville on board the "S.S. Northern Ranger".

Chapter 14
Carmanville Dec. 31 - Jan. 1

The bodies arrived at Carmanville on Sunday afternoon at 4 o'clock. On the way down from Old Perlican the Northern Ranger stopped at Musgrave Harbour where the casket containing the body of Otto Hicks was conveyed to shore by a committee of Orange Young Britons using Mr. Kenneth Abbott's motor boat. The burial was attended by the whole population.

At Carmanville the Rev. G.W. Case together with Constable J.S. Bath, and a committee from the Loyal Orange Lodge were at the coastal wharf to meet, and take delivery of the bodies. They were taken off the ship, and while still at the pier the officers, crew and passengers of the steamer sang "Nearer My God To Thee." Flags were flying quietly at half-mast at the Orange Hall, at the wharf and all over the settlement, while the bell of the United Church tolled. The bodies were conveyed from the wharf to the Orange Hall where the caskets were opened, identification made and remains conveyed to their homes.

The Goodyears' father and two sons were placed in the new home which they intended to move into in the New Year 1945. Their final resting place was in the family plot in The Salvation Army Cemetery.

The combined funeral services for Captain Chaulk and Mate Ellsworth were held from their homes to the United Church, which was crowded with sorrowing relatives and friends. The services were conducted by Rev. G.W. Case, assisted by Mr. Chesley Woolfrey and Adjutant Peach of The Salvation Army. Interment was at the United Church Cemetery. The funeral of John Goodyear and his two sons, Reginald and Charles was conducted by Adjutant Peach and assisted by Rev. G. Case, and Pastor Rideout. Interment was in the family plot in The Salvation Army Cemetery.

All the caskets were covered with wreaths, and the funerals were stated to be the saddest ever attended, and by the largest assembly of sympathetic friends in that part of the country. And so ended the tragic disaster of the schooner "Mollie" lost at Grate's Cove on December 20th, 1944 with all her crew of six men.

Chapter 15
Appreciation for Grate's Cove

There could be nothing but the highest praise for the indefatigable and devoted manner in which the people of Grate's Cove carried out the difficult and arduous task of searching for the bodies of the victims of this tragic accident. The people of Carmanville through Constable J.S. Bath sent a special message to acting Chief of Police Strange at St. John's requesting him to convey their grateful thanks to the people of Grate's Cove for their untiring efforts in searching for the bodies and to the Gerald S. Doyle News Bulletin for information supplied by the bulletins from time to time, and to the authorities for the transportation arrangements. Mrs. Nellie Chaulk, mother of Captain Ross Chaulk, also sent a special message of thanks both to the people of Grate's Cove and to all who had assisted in their terrible bereavement.

After the funeral services the next day the Gerald S. Doyle News Bulletin broadcast a message: "With the kind permission, and approval of Captain Snow a committee was formed and a contribution of $261.00 was raised from the officers, crew and passengers, which amount we are telegraphing today to Rev. G. W. Case, United Church Pastor at Carmanville for distribution where necessity calls, to the bereaved relatives of the men of the schooner "Mollie".....Sgd. E. Strangemore, W. Hounsell, J.P. Paddock.

Conclusion

Two poems written by two elderly and respected gentlemen of Carmanville sum up the general feeling and sorrow of the bereaved:

The Loss of the Mollie

1. Come bow your heads and listen,
   While a story I relate
   About the good ship Mollie;
   That met a saddening fate.

2. She left St. John's on Tuesday.
   December the nineteenth day,
   And we believe she reached a point
   Well out in Trinity Bay.

3. We have no facts to ascertain,
   What course she did pursue,
   But we believe she hove about,
   And steered back for Baccalieu.

4. The wind increased, the snow fell fast
   The Mollie made lee way,
   And came to grief in Grate's Cove Bight
   Before the break of day.
5. She had a stalwart crew of five,
   Yet on board there were six,
   One man from Musgrave Harbour,
   His name was Otto Hicks.
6. Ross Chaulk he was her captain.
   James Ellsworth was the mate.
   John Goodyear next with his two sons,
   The youngest twenty-eight.
7. The wind decreased, the snow cleared up,
   And wreckage was in sight.
   The men of Grate's Cove quickly saw
   What was the Mollie's plight.
8. The alarm was given a search was made,
   Along the rugged coast.
   But not a trace of life was found
   For all the crew was lost.
9. The seas ran high, but boats were manned,
   A continued search ensued,
   Until the bodies were taken
   From those waters cold and rude.
10. And when they were recovered,
    There was another call,
    And they were quickly taken
    To The Loyal Orange Hall.
11. And there prepared for burial,
    With the best that could be found,
    Awaiting for the "Ranger,"
    The ship that brought them down.
12. All friends at Grate's Cove did assist,
    They quickly saw the need;
    And all joined in to do their best,
    From every class and creed.
13. Our praise is only simple words,
    Yet we extend to you,
    Our grateful thanks from Carmanville,
    For your efforts brave and true.

14. It was on a Sunday evening,
    They were landed one by one.
    On the coastal wharf at Carmanville
    Just as the sun went down.

15. While Captain Snow and all onboard,
    With bared heads stood and sang.
    The Hymn, "Nearer My God To Thee,"
    As mournfully the Church bell rang.

16. And now those men are laid to rest,
    Within their narrow bed.
    Just think of them in Realms of bless,
    And not as souls now dead.

17. We all are sailing the sea of Time.
    Our journey here is brief,
    There will be storms we may escape,
    But not Time's ending Reef.

18. And to all our friends that sorrow,
    We commend you to God's care.
    No promise stands the test like His;
    He is always very near.

Composed by;
Mr. Willis Tulk,
Carmanville, Nfld. 1944

The Loss of the Schooner "Mollie"

1. Come all ye Newfoundlanders, and hear of this sad tale,
   About the Schooner "Mollie;" which foundered in a gale.
   On the nineteenth of December those men left St. John's, town;
   With joyful expectations were glad they were homeward bound.
   But the day was short and the night was long with snow and hail,
   The wind came in from the North East, and blew an awful gale.

2. A chilly mist enwrapped the dawn upon that fading morn;
   For in the darkness of the night a savage storm was born.
   A mighty whirling wind rushed fast toward that land of Death,
   It smote with sword of sharpest teeth, and with resistless breath,
   And terrible the sea that dashed on high with awful roar,
   'Twas there the "Mollie" met her doom on the rocks of Grate's Cove shore.

3. Oh God! Our helpless sailors, those men upon the wave,
   With wind and sea all lashing round, was there no power to save?
   Thou lookest down, O Mighty God, on passing scenes of woe,
   Grim Death which ends rich lives is not so dire a foe.
   But yet those dying, drowning cries ring in my ears the more,
   Re-echo from that Point of land, the coast of Grate's Cove shore.

4. But Hark! What is that muffled sound?, Me thinks I hear them pray,
   A prayer that none but God could hear on that cold stormy day.
   They might have prayed for human help, but none was very nigh,
   But prayer is surely answered and God took them home on high.
   So with that boundless mercy which comes from God alone,
   We leave them in His loving hands who were so far from home.

5. 'Twas there the "Mollie" went ashore, and all six men were drowned,
   The Grate's Cove men worked hard and all their bodies found.
   Our praise is due to those fine men, who worked both day and night,
   To get the bodies from the deep was met with our delight.
   Again we thank them one and all, and love them every one,
   God will reward them all when all their work is done.

6. The last day of December the "Ranger" hove in sight,
   With her flag half-mast, a single blast we knew that she was right.
   She came up in the Harbour, although it was but slow,
   The wind was light and frosty and but a little snow.
   She came in very easy when all was calm and blue,
   She tied up at the Coastal wharf and landed the "Mollie's" crew.

7. And when the dead were landed on that sad eventide,
   The crew and passengers lined the deck all on the Starboard side.
   "Nearer My God To Thee" they sang; while heads were bared and bowed,
   Our hearts did ache, many tears were shed all from that humble crew.
   And then the "Ranger" cast off lines and from the wharf did slip,
   As we bade adieu to the noble crew and passengers of that good ship.

8. And now our friends are sleeping within their narrow tomb,
   We'll meet again, we don't know when, it may be very soon.
   So dry your tears my sorrowing friends and face us with a smile,
   The Saviour said that He would come again, it's only a little while.
   And when all our work is done, and we the River cross,
   We'll meet our friends in the "Haven of Rest" where never a ship is lost.

Composed by: Mr. Kenneth Hicks,
Carmanville, Nfld.
(In his 74th year 1945)

Submitted by Mr. Hicks as a token of sympathy to Mrs. Nellie Chaulk in the sad loss of her son Skipper Ross.

And the following poem was composed by a Mrs. Avery of Grate's Cove in 1945:

The Wreck of the Schooner "Mollie"

1. 'Twas on a dear December night
   The schooner "Mollie" was lost;
   With all her crew and cargo too,
   Mid snow wind and frost.
2. Out from St. John's to Carmanville,
   Their home in Notre Dame Bay,
   A sturdy schooner and her crew
   Was lost in Trinity Bay.
3. Captain Ross Chaulk a fine young man,
   The captain of his ship
   With Otto Hicks, his boyhood friend,
   Decided to take the trip.
4. Now Otto had been overseas,
   The Navy was his choice.
   And he came home to spend some time
   But the wild seas took his life.
5. Mr. Goodyear and his two sons,
   Also comprised the crew;
   But they too met a watery grave
   Near Grate's Cove, this is true.
6. The seas were rough, but kind friends prayed
   And a calm came from above.
   Stout men in boats searched the wild sea,
   For the crew with hearts of love.
7. All rescued from the angry sea,
   Their bodies sent home once more
   So when the sea gives up its dead,
   We'll meet on Heaven's Shore.

The Loss of The Mollie

The following are the names of the crews who engaged in the search for the bodies:

Crew No. 1. Jeremiah Broderick, Peter Broderick, Isaac Broderick, John T. Broderick.

Crew No. 2. Daniel Duggan, George Martin, Leo Doyle, Daniel Doyle.

Crew No. 3. William J. Martin, Ingvauld Avery, Ben Avery, Reuben Stansford.

Crew No. 4. William H. Martin, Eli Martin, Vincent Duggan.

Crew No. 5. Wesley Snelgrove, Absalom Cooper, Sr. Levi Benson, Joseph Avery, John Vey.

Crew No. 6. Henry Meadus, George Meadus, Wesley Cooper, Abram Martin.

Crew No. 7. James Snelgrove, Simon Snelgrove, John Meadus, Daniel Vey.

Crew No. 8. Silas Lambert, William Lambert, Jacob Lambert.

Crew No. 9. Eli King, Stanley King, Joseph Benson, Frederick Lewis, Andrew Lewis.

Crew No. 10. Wilson Cooper, Archibald Barrett, Absalom Cooper, Jr.

Crew No. 11. Joseph Hodder, Absalom Hodder, Josiah Avery.

Crew No. 12. Benjamin Benson, Roland Doyle, Frank Doyle.

Crew No. 13. William B. Avery, Ernest Avery.

Otto Hicks, Musgrave Hr. Drowned in the schooner "Mollie" at Grate's Cove 20 Dec. 1944.

Capt. Ross Chaulk. "Mollie". Lost December 20, 1944, Grate's Cove, Nfld.

Mate of "Mollie" James Ellsworth. Loss Dec. 20, 1944, Grates Cove, Nfld.

The Goodyear family, Carmanville: Oswald, * Charles, * Reginald, * John, Mary. * Lost in "Mollie".

In the foreground, a short strip of shingle beach at the bottom of the gulch — near Grate's Cove.

One body was found in this part of the gulch.

Rocks where the schooner 'Mollie' is thought to have met her doom in heavy seas. Four bodies were recovered nearby.